Women's Writing

The later twentieth century saw a huge wave of academic interest in women's writing, which led to the rediscovery of neglected works from a wide range of genres, periods and languages. Many books that were immensely popular and influential in their own day are now studied again, both for their own sake and for what they reveal about the social, political and cultural conditions of their time. A pioneering resource in this area is Orlando: Women's Writing in the British Isles from the Beginnings to the Present (http://orlando.cambridge.org), which provides entries on authors' lives and writing careers, contextual material, timelines, sets of internal links, and bibliographies. Its editors have made a major contribution to the selection of the works reissued in this series within the Cambridge Library Collection, which focuses on non-fiction publications by women on a wide range of subjects from astronomy to biography, music to political economy, and education to prison reform.

Professional Women Upon Their Professions

Margaret Heitland (1860–1938), née Bateson, who became active in the suffrage movement, was the daughter of William Henry Bateson, Master of St John's College, Cambridge. In 1886 she moved to London to work as a journalist, joining in 1888 the staff on the magazine, *The Queen*, where she began its 'Women's employment department' feature the following year. She returned to Cambridge in 1901 upon her marriage to William Emerton Heitland, a Fellow of St John's, and she continued to be very active in the women's movement. This fascinating series of conversations with Victorian professional women first appeared in *The Queen* and was published in book form in 1895. Her aim was to offer inspiration and advice to young women seeking a career, and to demonstrate 'the intense happiness that merely being and doing *something* yields'. The wide range of professions represented include acting, dentistry, librarianship and stockbroking.

Cambridge University Press has long been a pioneer in the reissuing of out-of-print titles from its own backlist, producing digital reprints of books that are still sought after by scholars and students but could not be reprinted economically using traditional technology. The Cambridge Library Collection extends this activity to a wider range of books which are still of importance to researchers and professionals, either for the source material they contain, or as landmarks in the history of their academic discipline.

Drawing from the world-renowned collections in the Cambridge University Library and other partner libraries, and guided by the advice of experts in each subject area, Cambridge University Press is using state-of-the-art scanning machines in its own Printing House to capture the content of each book selected for inclusion. The files are processed to give a consistently clear, crisp image, and the books finished to the high quality standard for which the Press is recognised around the world. The latest print-on-demand technology ensures that the books will remain available indefinitely, and that orders for single or multiple copies can quickly be supplied.

The Cambridge Library Collection brings back to life books of enduring scholarly value (including out-of-copyright works originally issued by other publishers) across a wide range of disciplines in the humanities and social sciences and in science and technology.

Professional Women
Upon Their Professions

Conversations

MARGARET BATESON

CAMBRIDGE UNIVERSITY PRESS

Cambridge, New York, Melbourne, Madrid, Cape Town,
Singapore, São Paolo, Delhi, Mexico City

Published in the United States of America by Cambridge University Press, New York

www.cambridge.org
Information on this title: www.cambridge.org/9781108052528

© in this compilation Cambridge University Press 2012

This edition first published 1895
This digitally printed version 2012

ISBN 978-1-108-05252-8 Paperback

PROFESSIONAL WOMEN

UPON

THEIR PROFESSIONS.

CONVERSATIONS

RECORDED BY

MARGARET BATESON.

LONDON :

HORACE COX,

WINDSOR HOUSE, BREAM'S BUILDINGS, CHANCERY LANE, E.C.

—

1895.

LONDON:
PRINTED BY HORACE COX, WINDSOR HOUSE, BREAM'S BUILDINGS, E.C.

PREFACE.

In venturing to bring together between the covers of a book the records of conversations which were originally uttered for the benefit of readers of the *Queen* newspaper, I have been animated by a twofold hope.

Primarily my endeavour has been to show by the evidence of trusty witnesses what possibilities for happy labour women may expect to find in certain of the professions and avocations that are now open to them. By intercourse with some young, or at least youthful-minded, member of each profession, I have sought to learn what, in these years of our waning century, are the seeds of thought which are germinating in the professions, and will bear fruit in the time to come. It has formed no part of my project to converse with persons simply for the sake of their individual professional eminence, nor to tabulate the contents of this little volume upon the plan of a lions' tea-party, for such assemblages are habitually tiresome. To discover in each instance a person with living ideas and aspirations concerning her profession has been my sole aim. That I have also been fortunate enough to find persons of acknowledged professional distinction in those whose ideas are here set forth merely shows that the possessors of ideas are never suffered to tarry long in the background. For the

imperfect manner in which their ideas are set forth, I trust
that the ladies concerned may accept my apologies, together
with my thanks for their own extreme kindness and helpfulness, which have rendered my interpretation much less
imperfect than it would otherwise have been. That the
imperfections are still both numerous and apparent I have
the misfortune to be aware.

Beside the object of reflecting current professional
thought in a way that should rather suggest that thought
than exhaust it, I have implied that I had another hope.
And it was principally for the realisation of this other hope
that I chose the conversational method, despite the difficulties that I knew must attend it. I had before me the
image of some girl who has not yet found her niche in the
world. The world is before her where to choose; but she
would give much gratitude to anyone who would guide her
in her choice. But somehow there appears to be no mentor
at hand—no one even who can offer almost any suggestion.
A loneliness of spirit falls upon her that is all the more
intense because of the very excess of guidance with which
her infant and scholastic years were surrounded. Then she
was told every moment what was the duty of that moment;
now there is upon such matters a silence that may be felt.
True, that perhaps she need not do anything. Let her
gather the rosebuds. By all means let her gather them.
Let her not miss one, unless it be that some other may
pluck it. To be sweet-and-twenty, and to live romance—
what is the use of bringing the distinctions of committee
rooms and examiners' boards into terms of comparison with
the great privilege of youth ? " *Les émotions, c'est la
vie* " ; and who that is worthy the gift of life at all would

waste the glamour of life's June in musty study or in fusty office ? But for some June comes not, and she brings so many storms in her train for others that they are almost glad when she is gone. But gone she is, soon or late, for all. Then succeeds the time of reaction and of blankness; the time when the girl becomes aware how great are her capacities not only for emotion, but for thought and action, and how utterly non-existent are the opportunities for their development—at all events in that part of the social system in which she finds herself. The centre of feminine professional activity is for her so near and yet so far. She is indeed in sorry plight. Often, I am inclined to think, the plight of those who live with her at this period is scarcely less sorry. These, her sympathetic kinsfolk, are rendered indifferent advisers both by their limited experience of professional life and by the very ambition which they feel for the maiden's future. To them the choice for a young woman of good education and belongings lies between complete domestic obscurity on the one hand and the very highest distinctions that art or letters can offer on the other. If their Gwendolen Harleth cannot rival the artistic Klesmer of the day, why she must be content to become Mrs. Grandcourt. To write novels, but not to write the novel of the age; to write articles, but not to write for the *Nineteenth Century;* to act, but not at the Lyceum; to paint, but not for the Academy; to play, but not on the platform of St. James' Hall—these are possibilities which, until lately, have scarcely entered the provincial parental mind. A man, it is understood, may be very middling indeed, and no remarks made ; but not a woman.

And yet what happiness there is in being middling! It would be easy enough to write pages concerning the pleasures and the immunities that middling folk enjoy, but that would not be to my present purpose. What I would rather suggest is the intense happiness that merely being and doing *something* yields. "Do not trouble to suggest it," says the superior reader; "it has been a truism since the world began." Perhaps; but there are truisms which people forget are true. And the last couple of generations or so, which doomed women to inertia, alternating with amateurism, forgot this venerable truth because it had grown somewhat musty. Now that our truth has renewed its youth and has quaffed of Faust's phial, the world pays more heed to its existence. But many are sceptics still; many misdoubt whether, behind this truth's smiling face and beneath his jaunty apparel, there be more than a skeleton pretence of life. There is, in other words, many a parent who ignores that his daughter is obeying any law of life when she shakes off the tedium of his excellently-appointed home, and sets forth on her *Wanderjahr*, not knowing whither her feet shall take her. "Pooh!" says he to himself, half-irritated, half-perplexed, "the girl does not know when she is well off. She is leaving me out of sheer bravado, expecting to conquer the world. Well, she may conquer it," and he gives a self-satisfied smile, "being my daughter. And if she does, I shall be excessively proud and pleased. On the other hand, being only a girl, she may not. Well, in that event, if she has a particle of sense, she will return post-haste to take her share of the stalled ox at the family board." And then some phantom of the mind whispers to him, "What if your daughter is not sensible? What if she fail but return not, preferring a life of busy failure to a stagnation of idle success?" The idea is insufferable. "What!" he exclaims, "am I to be the father of a clerk in a counting-house, of a newspaper reporter, or of a fifth-rate actress? I should be the laughing-stock of my friends. No; I decline to let my daughter be a failure; she shall either be a genius—or a wife."

Hampered, then, as our maiden is in the solution of her life's problem by excessive ambition, coupled with insufficient suggestion on the part of her natural advisers, she is prone to seize eagerly upon any hint that comes to her in the form of chance conversation. She hears from Miss Smith that Miss Brown told her that the celebrated actress, Mme. X——, began her career as an artists' model. From that moment she thinks of artists' models with lively admiration. Then she reads somewhere that Mr. Walker, the novelist, would never have known what a genius he possessed for fiction had he not competed once for a guinea prize in *Rag Fair*. She fastens upon these undigested facts because none others are forthcoming, and the chances are, if she is a girl of spirit, and if the insipidity of her life has become unendurable, that she proceeds to take some desperately ill-advised step.

What the girl really wants is half-an-hour's talk with an experienced woman who has ideas to offer about the profession towards which the girl's own thoughts incline. Face to face with a woman who has succeeded herself, and who is generously wishful that others should emulate her success, the girl will obtain a stimulus and an encouragement that will be to her the much-needed stirrup-cup upon her long journey. It is for this reason that I have been emboldened to ask questions in the name of inquirers, whose needs I know if I know not them, and I have recorded the answers, not with the ability wherewith they were given me, but after the humble measure of my powers.

While in regard to my choice of professions I am bound to admit that I have followed a somewhat wayward fancy, omitting those concerning which it appeared to me that no specially new ideas were forthcoming, I shall not apologise for having generally dubbed professions various occupations that are not so classified in the narrower technical sense. I have, however, not cared to strain at the signification of the word, and have accounted as a profession any form of work which a woman is paid by the public, or entrusted by the public to do, and which she performs under that full sense of responsibility which we term the professional, in contradistinction to the amateurish spirit.

There is one respect, nevertheless, in which an apology is due. The profession of Journalism (which, except from the professional point of view, I would never willingly look at apart from Literature) numbers at least as many women with interesting ideas about their work as any other of the professions here represented. But for professional modesty I could put this opinion in a stronger form. It happens, my readers will perceive, to be the calling which I follow, and for this reason I found myself in an unforeseen and, I confess, ridiculous difficulty. I discovered that on this particular subject I wished to say something myself, and that this something made me, as it were, a choked-up speaking tube for any journalist who might care to express her thoughts through me. Under these circumstances I at last decided that it would be better to express my own poor thoughts truthfully than somebody else's far better ideas unveraciously.

The paper on "Journalism," I should add, is new, but "The Home Life of Professional Women" is an article which, after publication in the *Queen*, I have obtained permission to append for reasons which anyone who pays me the compliment of glancing at it will probably find sufficiently explained therein.

London ;

June, 1895.

CONTENTS.

xii Contents.

(From a photograph by Alfred Ellis, 20, Upper Baker-street.)

PROFESSIONAL WOMEN

THEIR PROFESSIONS.

———◦✦◦———

ACTING.

MISS FANNY BROUGH.

HOW DELIGHTFUL it must be to interview actresses!" is a remark people have often made to me, in that vague, indiscriminating way people have. As a matter of fact, it is not always delightful. There are actresses behind the footlights, beautiful, high-souled heroines, full of the loftiest emotions and the most amazing altruism, who on retiring to their dressing-rooms seem to shed their souls with their paint, and retain no ideas, no thoughts, no feelings; naught but a diminished beauty.

But to meet a fine actress who is also a clever woman, and, what is better, a large-hearted woman, I know of no pleasure more stimulating than this. Some few such actresses it has been my privilege to meet; and in the short but brilliant list I place high the name of Miss Fanny Brough. An admirable actress, as everybody agrees who can remember her Mrs. Egerton Bompas in "The Times," with its exquisite indications of the tenderness that may be hid in a worldly woman's nature; or who has seen her in such broadly laughable pieces as "The Magistrate," "The Late Lamented," "Our Flat," and "Dr. Bill." But, brilliant artist though she is, Miss Brough is something more, or at least something rarer than this. I scarcely know how to define the quality which distinguishes Miss Brough; but perhaps, if I were to call it her professional public spirit, I should most nearly indicate that which gives her an almost unique position amongst her fellow-actresses.   On the women's side she is practically, if not in name, the leader of the reforming party in the dramatic world.   For in the theatrical profession there is a movement, the counterpart of which we may observe in almost all other professions, for bringing the members into closer union for their mutual benefit, for closing the ranks against amateurs and idlers, and for regulating the system of admission and training.   The movement emanates from the Actors' Association, a society which has Sir Henry Irving for its president, and for vice-presidents Miss Ellen Terry, Mr. Lionel Brough (Miss Fanny Brough's uncle), Mr. Hare, Mr. Wilson Barrett, and Mr. Terriss. Miss Brough herself is a member of the council, and has her friends Miss Beatrice Lamb and Miss Carlotta Addison for colleagues on that body.

THE ACTORS' ASSOCIATION'S WORK.

It was fitting, then, that I should meet Miss Brough at the association's pleasant rooms in St. Martin's-lane.   How was the association getting on was the question naturally that sprang to my lips after Miss Brough had kindly bidden me ask whatever I wished to know.   "We are getting on; yes, certainly we are getting on, and our numbers have steadily increased during the year that is ending.   But we want what everybody wants nowadays—funds.   You see our subscription is very low, perhaps too low, but we wished to make the association useful to the poorest members of the profession, and so we fixed it at ten shillings."

"Why, the use of these club-rooms alone is worth more than that!" I exclaimed.   "Yes, as a mere club, these rooms, well warmed and lit, comfortably furnished, and in a central situation, are worth all the half-sovereign.   Actors and actresses can meet here (for the rooms are free to both sexes), and hear in conversation of many openings that they could not know of otherwise. But the association does a great deal more for its members than this.   Take the sanitary work, for instance.   There are theatres, and some of them important theatres, where the sanitation is very defective.   Should any member of our body make a complaint on this score, we inform the manager that a complaint has reached us, and we draw his attention to the matter in question.   Usually the defect is promptly remedied, but, should it not be, the association invites the sanitary authority to take the necessary action. There is nothing personal in such transactions, for we do not divulge the name of the complainant, and simply take up the affair as a corporate body acting on behalf of the profession. Similarly in this representative capacity we have been able to assist our members in all kinds of difficulties, often involving valuable legal advice, which the association's solicitors, Messrs. Bolton and Mote, generously give free of charge.

"In short, it seems to me," said I, drawing an illustration from my own profession, "that your association answers to the Society of Authors and the Writers' Club in one?" "Yes, I suppose we do. And I have not told you besides of our free register. Yet you would hardly believe that for some people all this is still not sufficient, and I have known members leave the association and then want to join it again when they have found themselves on the threshold of some expensive litigation. But that sort of behaviour is just a little too much!" And there was a good deal of fire in Miss Brough's keen grey eyes as she spoke of these penitents on the cheap. "We raised a special fund a year ago," she continued, "for the association, to which Mr. Alexander gave a very handsome cheque, and one or two others beside myself contributed. Lately, thanks to a successful benefit which the council arranged, under the auspices of our splendid president, Sir Henry Irving, who gave the Lyceum for the occasion, the Association was able to place a very satisfactory balance at our bank, and we have every reason now to feel we are slowly but surely making way towards future solid success."

"But is it not always an uphill struggle, Miss Brough, to induce people to unite for any non-personal cause, but especially to induce the women?" "Yes, especially the women," she answered regretfully. "They often say to me, 'It is very well for you, Miss Brough, who have climbed the ladder, to take all this trouble about the association, but I have my way to make. I cannot spare the time for it.' Well, it appears to me that it is a very short-sighted policy for a beginner not to avail herself of the help that union gives; and, perhaps, so far as I am concerned, it is not always quite such an easy matter to attend the council meeting every week, as I endeavour to do."

Seeing that Miss Brough, at the time I met her, was acting twice a day nearly every day in the week, I fancied this one engagement more might, to a less unselfish woman, appear just one too many.

THE CONSERVATOIRE SCHEME.

"Yes; I am still wishing we could have a national school of dramatic art," said my hostess, as we turned to another part of the subject. "I prefer, perhaps, to call it a Conservatoire, because it should be after the French pattern. The old stock companies have almost disappeared; Mr. Benson's company is about the only one that gives beginners the variety of practice they need, and that I had myself when, at the age of fourteen, I joined Charles Calvert's stock company in Manchester. That is one reason. Another is that the stage is being simply flooded with beginners. It is becoming a mere refuge for the destitute! You may smile, but it is true. Not a day but brings me a letter from somebody, to say that he has failed in his trade (whatever it may be) and thinks of taking to the stage. I try to keep pace with these letters and to answer them regularly, but it is very difficult. And suppose one of these persons goes on the stage? Imagine that our aspirant is a tall man, and knows that a manager is wanting some six-foot supers as soldiers. The beginner seizes his chance, and from that day he is good for nothing in the world. He will never return to his former pursuits; he is stage-struck. And the end of that man, unless he is just the *one* exception, is to become an idle, loafing, worthless fellow. For there is no idleness so demoralising as that of the actor who does not work.

"Look, too, at the injury done to our profession by the competition of these wealthy amateurs! I know many actresses—actresses of merit, mind you, not incapables—who are almost starving. But if they are to interview a manager successfully, they must be well dressed; they must look prosperous. A manager is only human after all; he is bound to consider the interests of his theatre, and he will not be disposed to do much for an actress who is obviously not getting on. The poor actress, though she may not actually be elbowed out by the richer amateur, finds existence made increasingly hard for her by this unlimited competition. Our

Conservatoire would at least close its doors against pupils who did not mean to work hard. But there would be no crippling of real talent; the cream would rise to the top as readily at the Conservatoire as anywhere else in this world."

PLAYS AND THE PUBLIC.

" You are a member of the Playgoers' Club, Miss Brough; that makes me feel sure you have views about plays as well as players." "I am interested in the Playgoers' Club, certainly, but not a member; the club only invite ladies as guests, not as members. I read a paper before the club on my special hobby, this school of dramatic art, and horribly nervous I was to find myself unprotected from my audience by footlights. About the public's taste in plays, it is useless, I think, either to talk or to theorise. Just now the public seems as though it could not have too much of the music-hall; and though such an artist as Dan Leno sends me into ecstasies, and I delight to see many of the most popular members of the music hall profession, the general run of the entertainments seems to me dull. For my own part, I should much prefer to be playing in a piece by Pinero or Grundy. The best of everything is about good enough for me, as for most other people in this world," she exclaimed, laughing, "but if the public likes farce, and the managers ask me to play farce, it is a case of needs must, and I play farce."

" And to my mind," I interposed, " it is a greater distinction to make something out of nothing than to act a part that would be interesting anyhow. But do you think the critics have much to do in affecting the success or failure of plays?" "No, not much; that is to say, critics can never 'boom' a piece into a success, but they may destroy a piece that the public has not definitely made up its mind to like. The public's taste is the real thing, and it is a factor about which it is useless to argue. I never listen to explanations about unlucky theatres, or bad weather, or depression of trade, or any of the other excuses people make for a failure, and if I should ever become a manager (as some of my friends try to induce me) I shall simply be guided in the matter of plays by the answer to the question—Does the public like the play or not?"

The riddle of public taste partly solved itself for me as I thought of Miss Brough's success, earned by long and toilsome years. There remained another puzzle, How had those years left Miss Brough her enthusiasms, her human sympathy, her generosity? I know not. There are still miracles in life.

MRS. MARY DAVIES.

(From a photograph by Messrs. Elliott & Fry, Baker-street.)

SINGING.

MRS. MARY DAVIES.

THE exponents of the arts, commonly so designated—music, painting, and the drama—are often artists in the first place, and in the second, and in the third. They do not begin to be human beings while they are here below. The crowd goes jostling past them, eagerly talking the talk of the hour, but they see and hear it not. Sometimes this attitude of aloofness seems rather fine in its uncommonness; oftener it looks merely selfish and inhuman. It would be pleasant to say that this attitude was exclusively adopted by the small folks, who might excusably focus their limited powers of intellect upon their peculiar handiwork. But it is not so; for there have been several of the greatest artists who have lived to themselves and their work alone, sparing no fraction of attention to the affairs that concern others. These, however, are not the generality, and, as a rule, we find in the highest grades artists who are not mere embodiments of the artistic temperament, but practical human beings, whose minds are large and hospitable enough to entertain ideas that have as much to do with human happiness as with the advancement of their particular art. As I write these words, I think especially of Mrs. Mary Davies, for I do not know any artist of equal distinction in whom this quality of mental hospitality is more strongly developed. Unfortunately, my allotted space is less hospitable, and I cannot therefore speak of the many subjects other than music in which Mrs. Davies is interested, but must content myself with saying that very little that concerns the welfare of women is alien to her. However, music alone was the mission which took me one day to the home of this delightful singer. And it was of music that we immediately fell a-talking, for as Mrs. Davies entered the room, bringing with her from a concert a bouquet of splendid tawny chrysanthemums which I admired, she said immediately, "Yes, are not they lovely? But to me their chief merit is that they have not much scent."

I looked an interrogation. "Because," she continued, "we singers are all agreed that strong-smelling flowers are injurious to the voice. Sims Reeves, for instance, will never sing with a sweet-scented flower in his buttonhole." Then, after a pause, she inquired, "And what is it you would like me to tell you? About singing as a profession?" "If you would," I replied; "and more particularly what curriculum you would recommend for a girl who hopes eventually to sing in public."

A SINGER'S PREPARATION.

"I should scarcely," said Mrs. Davies, "wish to say that the curriculum I myself underwent is the best, but it is certainly one of the best. The Royal Academy of Music was my training school. I studied there for five years, learning singing chiefly from Mr. Randegger, and, indeed, I continued to take lessons from him for a long while after the regular course was finished. There is always something more to be learnt in singing—or to be unlearnt," she added, with a smile.

"And what is the cost of a musical training?" "At the Royal Academy of Music, thirty guineas a year; at the Royal College of Music, forty guineas. But a first-rate training, such as may be obtained at either of these institutions, will not do everything. Attention to hygiene I consider almost equally important, and on this account I wish very much that there were more well-managed homes for musical students in London, where the rules of health could receive proper attention. As you perhaps know, I am a great believer in temperance, and consider stimulants injurious to the voice. Proper and sufficient food and a regular mode of life are absolutely necessary for singers, especially when they are young and the voice is just developing. I really attribute my own excellent health to the régime under which I lived in my childhood, for as a child I was very delicate."

"I suppose singing itself often makes people stronger?" "Undoubtedly; one learns to breathe properly in singing. For this reason I think it ought to be taught in all schools, though the nasal singing of Cockney children may be rather distressing to those who live near Board Schools. But to revert to our student of singing. I should recommend her to practise also light gymnastic exercises. On no account should she sing in public during her training period, for the nervous strain upon a girl who has probably not made all her growth is very trying."

How to Gain a Hearing,

"When did you first sing in public, Mrs. Davies?" I asked. " Oh, I may say that I have sung in public ever since I was ten. Still, I do not consider that I made my regular *début* until after my training at the Academy. And horribly nervous I was both then and for long afterwards. One often hears people use the expression about wishing they could sink into the ground. Well, I have often longed for the floor of the platform to open and swallow me up. But I was certainly fortunate in my start, for I had a most excellent friend in Mr. Brinley Richards, who introduced and recommended me in various quarters. I began by singing at Welsh concerts."

" Your home was in Wales, I believe?" " No, that is a mistake. I was born in London, but of Welsh parents, and I have always associated a great deal with my countrymen, and attended the Welsh Church. So that it was natural I should begin by singing at Welsh concerts, and in particular at Mr. Brinley Richards'. In this way my name gradually became known, and persons who had heard me came to invite me to sing at other concerts."

How a Good Agent Helps.

·I asked Mrs. Davies whether she used to employ an agent to conduct these negotiations. " No," she answered, " I had no agent in those days.

" Do you believe that agents can be of much service?" " Certainly; of great service—good agents, of course. They are helpful in many ways. Mind, an agent cannot do everything. A girl, to begin with, must bring a good recommendation from her singing teacher. That is the first and best step to take; then probably the agent will hear her sing. If she shows promise, he will submit her name to musical societies wishing for performers. The agent is naturally of service in arranging terms. He can advise the neophyte what terms she would be wise in demanding or accepting, and he can tell her about the position in the musical world of the societies that wish to engage her. Under some circumstances it may be worth while for a beginner to accept modest terms in return for the distinction of performing under good auspices."

" Now what are the agent's usual terms ?"   " Ten per cent. on the total sum received. The vocalist gets a specified remuneration for singing, which includes travelling and all other expenses. In some cases, as you may suppose, the expenses involved make a serious hole in a singer's earnings."

The Dress Question.

" Dress, for instance," I murmured.   " Ah ! dress," said Mrs. Davies, with something like a sigh.   " How I sometimes envy a man, who doesn't need to trouble about costume. The amount of time and thought, as well as expense, that it entails ! And I verily believe there is no place in the world so dirty or so ruinous to a gown as a concert platform. But I admit that the singer must be well dressed ; the public expects it. All the same, I do not hold with over gorgeousness. I am no believer in the principle of ' spending to get.' And I do not think that I ever had prettier or more becoming concert gowns than those I wore in early days, which my mother used to make for me." As the dress question is really a serious one to the feminine performer, I noticed these remarks with much satisfaction, for Mrs. Mary Davies's mastery of the graceful art of dress is known to everybody who has an eye for such matters.

Concert Touring.

Then we went on to discuss the mapping out of the musical year.

" In London the dullest time of the year is July and August. But then the singers can go on tour to the seaside towns, such as Southport, Llandudno, Rhyl, &c.; and there are various other resorts, such as Bournemouth, which may be visited in the winter months. I have sometimes been surprised at the number of concerts that are given in these seaside places. I recently found myself at Southsea when six concerts were taking place simultaneously, and all well attended."

"With regard to audiences: do you find they are much the same?" "Oh, not at all! There are the greatest possible differences. The audiences that I should say were most appreciative are in Lancashire, Yorkshire, and Staffordshire. South of that region I should say there is less feeling for music, though Birmingham no doubt is musical."

"And what about the far North—Scotland, the land of the ballad?" "The Scots are appreciative of good music, but they are extremely critical. With regard to their ballads, many of them are of extraordinary beauty. But nearly every nation has some fine ballads. It is almost a pity that many singers confine their attention so exclusively to a few familiar ballads, when there are so many almost equally beautiful that are scarcely known. I wish that some of them could be revived."

I wish so, too, and I hope that they may be sung by Mary Davies, for a ballad sung by her is the perfection of poetry in music.

PAINTING.

MRS. ERNEST NORMAND (HENRIETTA RAE).

A MENTAL ATTITUDE of discouragement would have been becoming. I felt that, as I journeyed southwards towards the heights of Gipsy Hill. For I was going to consult Mrs. Normand upon the possibilities that the artist's life holds for women, and there, in my pocket, was a letter in which Mrs. Normand told me in so many words that the possibilities were of the meagrest. I took out the letter again, thinking, as one does, to find some little grain of comfort that had gone unnoticed at first. But no; the sentences remained uncheering.

" I must tell you," she wrote, " that I never can conscientiously hold out the flattering hopes of success for women in art that most people seem to expect from me. I have seen so many hundreds of girls start in the race with more than the average meed of success in the preliminary stages of art tuition, only to fall short entirely when opposed by the difficulties of original creation, that I have come to the conclusion that the sex generally labours under the disadvantage of some curious inability to rise above mediocrity in art, as also in musical creative composition. Every art school in the world is thronged with women in the proportion of two-thirds women to one-third men. The women take all the prizes in the preliminary stages, and one hears nothing of them afterwards. The men, even if they do not reach the goal they start for, nearly all produce competent work in some groove or another, and many of them attain celebrity. Nearly all the R.A.'s and A.R.A.'s (figure painters) were students at the Academy or South Kensington, and out of the whole host of women who worked side by side with them, you can count on the fingers of one hand those who have attained even to mediocrity. These statistics are not such as to lead a competent adviser to hold out great hopes for the future."

Undoubtedly I ought to have felt discouraged. Yet somehow I

MRS. ERNEST NORMAND.

(Photographed by H. T. Reed, 16, Tottenham-court-road.)

was much more enlivened by the prospect of seeing one woman who had succeeded, than depressed by the thought of all that "host" who had failed with greater or less moderation. For it seemed to me that if those multitudinous young ladies had cared greatly to increase the number of big pictures in the world, they would certainly not have allowed their sex or anything else to stand in the way; and if, after all, they had been neither chagrined or bored with leading a life of indistinction, nobody need be concerned. So I arrived at the studio ready to hear the worst with unruffled calm.

PREPARING FOR THE ACADEMY.

But first there was more to see than to hear. For on entering the studio, whither Mrs. Normand led me through the garden that slopes upward from a pretty house, I found Mr. Normand seated before a vast canvas, making the most of the lingering daylight. He was working on the figure of a child, for which a sunny haired· little girl posed with trained immobility. He greeted me as amiably as if an interruption were· quite the most agreeable circumstance that could befall an artist within three weeks of sending-in day. Mrs. Normand, with equal good nature, allowed me to look at her picture for the year, "Apollo and Daphnè." Apollo, draped in a leopard skin (after a manner that permits the artist to exhibit her certainty of touch in painting the figure), is pleading his cause rather forcibly with Daphne, who turns towards him in an attitude half terrified, half supplicating. The sea lies blue and still beyond them. It is dramatic, effective, and probably—using the adjective in the best sense—the most ambitious work that Mrs. Normand has yet attempted. It means that she is determined to go forward in spite of the circumstance that a large section of the public would be quite content if she stood still.

"I am prepared," she said, "to hear that some people are disappointed with it. They will complain that it is not so 'pretty' as some of my other pictures. They will wish it were more like that (indicating with her hand the jewelled loveliness of " Zephyrus wooing Flora "). That is the worst of ever painting pretty pictures. The public will not let one do anything else. However, it really doesn't do to think about the public."

THE ARTIST AS CRITIC.

"Nor about the critics?" I put in with light-hearted malice, not being of that company.

" Well, not too much" was the reply. "But I must say I have sometimes profited by press criticism, even when it has seemed at the time terribly severe."

And then Mr. Normand, who had now put aside his brushes, joined in the talk. The general mass of inept and incompetent criticism found him, of course, indifferent; but he could not quite understand why serious pictures were so often looked upon as fair game for the journalistic joker. He had remonstrated once with a critic on the subject. The critic was appraising the Academy. He began with the big pictures of the R.A.'s, and, without committing himself to an opinion, described the subject of each masterpiece with grave propriety. But as soon as he came to Mrs. Normand's " Ariadne deserted by Theseus " he gave himself over to facetiousness.

"Happening to meet him," Mr Normand continued, " I asked him why he had turned my wife's picture into ridicule. 'My dear fellow,' he said, 'if you only knew how dull and unreadable the column would have been without those little jokes, I am sure you would not have begrudged them me. Why, they just lightened up the whole affair!' So I suppose we must submit. *Punch*, too, makes great fun of us, but his jokes are always good natured. Do you remember the parody of 'Eurydice Sinking Back into Hades'? It was at the time when Horsley made his protest against women studying from the nude; and *Punch* represented Eurydice throwing herself back in the attitude of the picture, while she pulled violently at Horsley's door-bell to call his attention to her scanty attire."

It occurred to me that artists were more awkwardly placed than most of us in being compelled to oblige three sets of people—the public, the critics, and fellow artists. To this both Mr. and Mrs. Normand assented, declaring, however, that they painted chiefly for the approbation of their fellow artists.

"An artist's criticisms are the only ones worth heeding," said Mr. Normand. "It was the great advantage of living in the Holland Park-road, as we used to do, that we could show our work to others. We benefited, in particular, by being neighbours of Sir Frederick Leighton. He used to come in and look at the pictures and tell us what was wrong with them. I assure you, after his visits, we always wondered what in the world had induced us to take to painting." "Yes, we used indeed," Mrs. Normand chimed in, rather dolefully. "Only he criticised, of course, in the most delightful way, and although the immediate effect of his criticism may have been depressing, we learnt much that we could not have acquired under any other circumstances."

"All the same," Mr. Normand wound up this matter by saying, " it would not do for us to become newspaper critics of each other's work. No; it would not do at all."

The Woman-Artist Question.

We drifted then into a three-cornered chat on the woman question; or, rather, on that part of it which Mrs. Normand's letter had touched.

" You scarcely expected me to say that the outlook for women artists was very brilliant at present, did you?" Mrs. Normand questioned. I admitted that I had scarcely formed any definite expectation, but that I had hoped, perhaps, she would recommend some particular course of training by which better results might be obtained. But I found that both Mrs. Normand and her husband were rather opposed to particular courses of training, looking upon recognised schools as affording encouragement to a number of incompetent students, girls especially.

" Girls," said Mr. Normand, " attend these schools in large numbers, without seriously intending to take to art as a career, and being naturally, I think, more industrious and conscientious than men, they do remarkably well as students. The cleverer ones manage to take prizes, and even the duller ones can be prepared just up to a certain standard of requirement. What we want is a system for reducing the number of women art students at the Academy and other art centres, not for increasing it. We want to weed out the incompetent girls, and the girls who are not resolutely determined to become artists. For after the student period the majority show no concentration of purpose, and they have filled vacancies in the schools that should have been occupied by others who could have made better use of the opportunity.

Mind, I do not mean to say there are not many men who fail, who are mediocre all their lives. But, at all events, it is not usually for want of serious endeavour. In becoming artists they know that they must do their best; for their career and reputation, if not their livelihood, are at stake. With a woman it is different. She says to herself, If I fail, there is always the possibility of marriage.' Social temptations, too, are a great snare. How many women will work steadily at a night school—as they ought to do if they mean to get on—when invitations to parties come in the way?"

"Yes," said Mrs. Normand, "I am very fond of social entertainments myself, and there are a great many pleasant gatherings I would like to go to. Only I should not be able to work next day after being up late at night; and art, I can assure you, demands anyhow great physical strength. It is too exhausting for most women. I take no small credit to myself," she added with a smile, "for having accomplished even as much as I have."

Then Mrs. Normand asked why, if women had meant to be artists, they had not become good landscape painters long ere this, for no difficulty about models interfered with them in that direction. To this question I daresay some satisfactory reply exists, but it escaped me at the moment, so I reverted to the question of training.

Before studying in the Academy School, Mrs. Normand said she had learnt most from studying at Hatherley's School and at the British Museum. "We learnt as best we could at the British Museum; it was simply a case of the survival of the fittest."

"Well," interposed her husband, "the person who really teaches one is not the professor but the best pupil in the class. Everyone tries to bring him or herself up to the standard of the cleverest pupil, and it simply depends on how clever that pupil is, how high the standard of the school becomes. Later in life one can teach and criticise oneself. In the early days one is simply fumbling in the dark. But with experience one becomes one's own teacher and severest critic."

Mr. Normand afterwards told me a great deal—*àpropos* of the important picture on which I found him engaged—about light and shade, values, and many other matters that the untrained spectator but dimly apprehends. However, I dare not digress from the feminine side of things. And I take pleasure in saying in this regard, that both Mr. and Mrs. Normand spoke in the most generous terms of the genius and distinction of many individual women artists, and notably of such as Lady Butler, Miss Clara Montalba, Mrs. Lea Merritt, Mrs. Tadema, Mrs. Swynnerton, Mrs. Adrian Stokes, and Mrs. Stanhope Forbes.

To the average young lady seeking a career with palette and brush, their attitude is nevertheless dissuasive. Mrs. Normand meets the maiden with a frank " Don't;" and Mr. Normand perhaps does much the same thing in suggesting that she should put this question to herself, " When I have mastered the language of art, have I anything to say in it that will interest others? "

ILLUSTRATION.

MISS C. M. DEMAIN HAMMOND.

THE DEMOCRATIC tendencies of our time, it is occasionally assumed, have entailed nothing but loss to artists. They have entailed loss to members of certain classes of artists, possibly. The patron of artists is now no longer the millionaire or the influential nobleman, for both the noble and the man of money have been outbidden by a stronger and a wealthier patron than they—the people. By this transfer of the seat of patronage, the painter and the sculptor suffer perhaps, though it would not be easy to offer convincing proof of the supposition. But, whether painter and sculptor lose or not, there can be no question that an artist of another class gains, and gains enormously, and will continue, so far as can be foreseen, to gain for an indefinite length of time to come. This is the illustrator.

The people demand to be informed and entertained; but informed directly, briefly; entertained unambiguously, visibly. The written word can scarcely carry its meaning to the mind of our new patron with adequate promptness; our patron yawns whilst the instruction and amusement are in process of conveyance. The artist in black and white is the only man who can tell anything quickly enough, and the novelist, essayist, journalist are all compelled to ask his help in communicating what they have to say to the people. The illustrator, then, has enough to do.

Strange is it that women who gladly sketch landscapes, gladly paint portraits, gladly pursue art—and not by any means always for art's sake alone—should scarcely yet have sought the popularity, fame, and fortune which reward successful endeavour in black and white draughtsmanship. How many are the women who illustrate our English magazines, weekly and daily papers? With the exception of fashion artists (and I am not dealing with them

MISS C. M. DEMAIN HAMMOND.

(From a pen and ink portrait by Miss Gertrude D. Hammond.)

on the present occasion), surely the number is most limited. I believe, but should be glad to be corrected, that they could be told off on the fingers of both hands. Why is it that women are missing this magnificent opportunity? I have asked myself. And I have answered myself that it is partly the fault of our training schools of art, where the students of either sex are too seldom directed towards this end, and that it is partly the fault of women in not exerting more power of initiative for their own behoof.

The · Making of a Black and White Artist.

In order, however, that this absence of suggestion should no longer be pleaded as an obstacle, I sought advice and information from Miss Christina Demain Hammond, who, with her sister, occupies a place of assured distinction among illustrators. I asked her, so soon as she had permitted me to establish myself in a sunny corner of her studio home at Hammersmith, what would be her advice to beginners?

Miss Hammond met my request with perfect frankness. " I cannot," she said, " suggest any better course than the one we took, my sister and I. We knew that we should have occasion to earn our own living, and having some talent for art, we determined to direct it towards illustration. We began, then, by attending the Lambeth School of Art, where, as you know, there was a most admirable teacher, Mr. Smith, who has lately died. It was Mr. Smith's method to encourage the pupils to make sketches of each other when the regular lesson was over. We were allowed to make these practice studies in any medium, and we drew pencil sketches of each other in the attitudes that seemed most characteristic. I consider that I derived great benefit from this kind of work. It taught us self-reliance and independence in the selection of pose and treatment. Later I also attended Mr. Brown's classes at Westminster for the nude, a knowledge of which is indispensable, of course for such work as mine, dealing chiefly with the human figure. Women can obtain no opportunity for such study at the Royal Academy, the schools of which I had entered on leaving Lambeth."

" You had not been long at the Academy I suppose when you began to receive commissions?" "No," said Miss Hammond.

" But artistic employment cannot be counted on with the certainty of many others.   One may be given some little order, and then there may be a long interval without one; then several may come all together.   An artist's earnings at the start are most precarious. But my first work of a settled character was for the *Detroit Free Press*, of which Mr. Barr is the editor.   I still draw for the paper. Last year I illustrated a reprint of Miss Edgeworth's " Castle Rackrent " and " The Absentee " for Messrs. Macmillan, which appeared early this year, and has been very favourably reviewed, and also a reprint of Marmontel's " Contes Moraux " for Mr. George Allen, which is about to appear at once.   I have in hand three more books, two more volumes of Miss Edgeworth's tales for Messrs. Macmillan, and for Mr. Allen a well-known English classic of the eighteenth century, the name of which I am not at liberty to give at present.   But perhaps you might like to see some of my things?"

Favourite Subjects and Methods.

Needless to say I *did* like; so Miss Hammond left, to return immediately with a big scrap-book, paged with proofs of engravings and process-blocks.   Many of the drawings (those especially that had appeared in the *Detroit Free Press* and *Pick-me-up*) were humorous, and displayed a strong grasp of the typical features in certain classes of mankind.

" I am always observing people," said Miss Hammond in explanation.   " Some artists, I suppose, do not care to notice their fellow-creatures in the streets and omnibuses, and so forth; at least I can only account in that way for the fact that so many women, for instance, can paint a portrait compared with the few who draw illustrations.   In black and white work, too, the artist cannot copy a model exactly."

" How do you manage about models ; surely you require some ? "

" Oh yes, I have models usually for my men's and women's figures, but the face and the expression I draw from the ideal that I imagine the author had in his mind.   When I am illustrating a story, I read the tale first, and as I read, I see the people all before me, and then I draw them to illustrate the moments of the story that I think most effective.   But I cannot be sure that I see the author's creations aright."

We were looking, as the artist said this, at the drawings made by

the two sisters for Mr. Kipling's "Badalia Herodsfoot," which to
the thinking of most readers reproduce with singular vigour the
principal figures in that grim study of East-end life.

"Here at least," I said, "you have certainly done justice to the
novelist's intentions."

"Well, I have reason to think Mr. Kipling was pleased," Miss
Hammond replied, modestly, "for my sister and I received several
flattering verbal messages about the drawings, which, indeed, I
believe are now in the author's possession. This was all the more
gratifying to us as we knew that amongst some of the journalistic
fraternity it was anticipated we should fail with such a strong
subject. The 'Badalia' drawings brought us another interesting
order. Mr. Robert Buchanan asked us to do two illustrations for
his poems, and afterwards wrote that he liked them extremely."

And then I asked Miss Hammond what she advised about
methods. Was it necessary to understand all the various methods
of artistic reproduction? "No, I hardly think so," she answered.
"One learns by experience what method of treatment it is necessary to adopt. Personally, I prefer pen-and-ink drawing, and
being extremely fond of pure line I avoid 'wash, which seems to
allow one to 'fluke' difficulties. I am seldom pleased with the
effect of engraving upon my work. I would far sooner have
my drawing reproduced by process just as it is, without the help
of an intermediary."

In reply to a further question concerning her present work, Miss
Hammond told me that she had done a great deal for Messrs.
Cassell's publications, and had lately been drawing for the *Idler*.
She was also about to try her hand at advertisement posters, in
execution of an order for Sir Joseph Causton and Co. "This is
quite an experiment," she added, "for one has to allow enormously
for enlargement from the original drawing, and the lines cannot be
too simple or too clear."

Pros and Cons of the Career.

"You would say then, Miss Hammond, that the career you have
adopted offers capital chances to women?" "Well, there seems
to be no lack at present; but I wonder whether illustration will
continue to grow in popularity at its present rate? Anyhow, we
do not want the profession to become overcrowded."

"What is your opinion, Miss Hammond, about the idea that has resulted in the formation of the Black and White Society "?

"Personally, I sympathise with the movement, although I was unable to attend the preliminary meeting. I believe the society might do for illustrators the same kind of work that the Authors' Society does for literary people. It might help beginners to make satisfactory terms for their work, and possibly establish some fixed minimum rate of pay. Prices now vary— and doubtless will continue to vary—according to the character and position of the publication or publisher, and also somewhat according to the name and reputation of the artist. One man will get as much as ten guineas for a half-page drawing, while another, who is not well known, may get two guineas or three. Payment is regulated, I think, even more by name and standing than by merit. As for the beginner, he or she has no better means of ascertaining the value of his work than to learn what his friends in the same line are receiving—which is more easily said than done. The inequalities and disparities cannot, of course, be done away with, but they might be modified, so as to bear less hardly on those who are at present without competent advisers."

"But, even under favourable conditions, illustration is tolerably hard work, I imagine "?

"It is arduous in the sense of allowing one scarcely any holidays. Newspapers, as you know, are always in a hurry, and I pride myself on doing my work up to time. But if I had not required to earn money at once, I should have preferred to paint pictures. Perhaps I may be able to fulfil my early ambition some day—who knows ? "

For Miss Demain Hammond, like so many other persons of fewer gifts, draws more pleasure from her " Madonna of the Future." her unachieved masterpiece, than from all the successes of the present.

MISS A. J. COOPER.

(Photograph by J. W. Beaufort, Birmingham.)

EDUCATION.

MISS A. J. COOPER.

WHY HAVE I NOT HEADED THIS INTERVIEW "High School Teaching," since my talk was with the distinguished Head Mistress of the Edgbaston High School for Girls—and one of the most distinguished Head Mistresses, be it added, of all who have shed honour on this department of the teacher's calling? For this reason; High School teaching is in the still waters. It has had its days of storm and stress, but they were a quarter of a century ago, and to-day it is in the position of the ideally respectable lady whose doings call for no remark. That the High School system offers yet a perfect education, no woman connected with that system would probably allow me to say. To live in an unbetterable world would be too dreary. And, personally, I am not disposed to affirm that the High School system realises *the* ideal. But I am prepared to say that approximately, and, allowing for human imperfections, it realises *an* ideal, and that a high one. Its ideal, I take it, is, if reduced to very few words, to offer to girls the most stimulating and the most comprehensive means of intellectual development possible.

The offer is made to young women of every natural temperament and of every class. Inevitably it is accepted most readily by girls of that class which, on the whole, most values intellectual development—the middle class. But, we ask ourselves, what of the others; what of those whose disposition or social condition is never likely to take them among things abstractly mental, who yet most sorely need education? Can nothing be done to make girls of this class (and girls of the higher classes, too, for that matter) more reasonable women, women with a better understanding of the world they live in, and more capable of turning their abilities to account in the practical callings and crafts?

Questions such as these have been fermenting latterly in the minds of many, and will no doubt receive an answer commensurate with their importance when the Secondary Education Commission, of which Mrs. Henry Sidgwick and Mrs. Bryant are members, issues its report.

We can hardly employ the period of waiting better than by considering what manner of answer is given by a lady who is an educationalist of wide vision even before she is a High School Mistress—Miss Cooper.

THE HIGH SCHOOL TEACHER.

Nevertheless, when I was fortunate enough to find Miss Cooper in London on a brief visit, it was impossible not to make High School teaching the first subject of inquiry. Miss Cooper put the *pros* and *cons.* impartially. On the *pro* side, Miss Cooper placed regularity of hours of work and ample holidays. To the *con.* side must be set the increasing competition, the long and expensive training (for both University and Training College qualifications are now in request), and the low salaries. About this matter of salaries Miss Cooper is especially concerned, having studied it exhaustively.

" The minimum salary," she observed, " at which I should like an assistant mistress to begin is £100. This should rise to at least £120 or £130. With us at Edgbaston no teacher begins at less than £100, and our salaries are higher than those usual in day schools. But I name £120 because it is the least on which a woman can hope to save money against old age."

I asked how much Miss Cooper would expect the teacher to save. " A really well paid teacher, if she lived very carefully and economically might lay by enough to purchase a pension of £80 a year—that would be about the least she could live on. I admit it would be difficult to save so much. Teachers require to live generously, both physically and intellectually. Many, too, have relations dependent on them, whose claims I am not one to overlook."

"The High School teacher is more speedily superannuated than most people, is not she?" I inquired ; adding tentatively, " after forty, I suppose, she would hardly have much chance of a new post?"   " No," said Miss Cooper ; " but that would not be entirely on account of her age. It would be felt that if she were a capable teacher she would have secured a head-mistress-ship by that time of life."

"Then," said I, "if the field of high school teaching is already so over-full, what of other fields? Are teachers altogether too many?" I found that, half by chance, I had touched on the subject that was uppermost in Miss Cooper's mind.

SECONDARY AND HIGHER GRADE TEACHING.

"No," replied the head mistress, "there are not too many teachers in all departments. There is one department in which there is a distinct opening for highly educated women—in which I have good reason to believe that before long there will be a very wide opening. I am referring to Elementary Higher Grade Schools. I am doing what I can now to persuade girls who have received a high school education to turn their attention in this direction. A girl, after she leaves school, ought, with a little special teaching, to be able to pass the Queen's Scholarship examination. After this two courses are open to her—(1) to become a student at a Residential Training College; (2) to go through the two years' course (which I hope may be raised eventually to three years) at the Day Training College. The second plan I recommend by preference, and the expense would be met by the Queen's Scholarship. She might go through a course of pupil teachership before taking the Queen's Scholarship, but this is not absolutely necessary."

"And then our ex-High School girl is to find her career in an Elementary School?" "Yes, but in one of the Higher Grade schools." Then, after a pause, Miss Cooper continued:
"We are on the eve of great developments. We shall be called upon shortly, it is revealing no secret, to reconstruct, or, shall we say, extend our system of secondary education. It is necessary to provide a better link than at present exists between the elementary school and the high school. The question is, what kind of education is that to be?"

THE UNION OF MIND AND HAND.

"Is it to be a more technical education?" I asked. "In a measure, I hope it may. As it is a subject to which I have given a good deal of thought, I will tell you my own ideas.   I feel that intellectual and technical education have too long been carried on along parallel lines which never meet.   They are both excellent in themselves, but would be more than twice as valuable if they were married to each other.   We need the one to help the other. To explain : in my ideal secondary school I should teach physics, elementary physiology and chemistry, with such practical sub-jects as cookery and laundrywork.   I should deal with history, beginning with the history of great men and the history of the locality, and then let the subject spread outwards, proceeding, you see, from what is near towards the more remote.   With needle-work, similarly, I should couple the principles of design, for I go so far as to say that the art of needlework would have been studied to better purpose if design had been as thoroughly taught as technique.   Bookkeeping is too useful a subject to be omitted."

" But you would not confine this curriculum, I imagine, to the Higher Grade schools ?   It is what so many other girls need."

" Yes ; but I think we could most wisely begin with girls, say of twelve, who have finished the ordinary elementary school course.   I should like such a system to spread to the secondary schools.   How far it might affect the higher schools it is too early to predict."

Miss Cooper, I ought to add, spoke in appreciative terms of the education now given at Higher Grade girls' schools, and thought it very good of its kind ; but she was, at the same time, of opinion that the kind was too purely literary for the needs of the pupils.   Concerning secondary schools proper, Miss Cooper complained that there were not enough of them.   " And," she went on to say, " I am afraid the teachers are sometimes badly paid.   You, perhaps, know that an endowed secondary school has a fixed endowment, besides its receipts from fees.   Let us suppose that the school is a good one, and the numbers increase. The endowment remains the same, consequently there is less to apportion to each teacher when more teachers are required.   For my own part, I would suggest that the fees should be made suffi-ciently high at the outset, so that there might be something in hand against the day of larger numbers.   Otherwise, it would be better to have bigger classes and fewer teachers, than that the latter should be underpaid."

OTHER POINTS PEDAGOGIC.

Afterwards we talked about other methods of teaching. The governess, Miss Cooper was not at all disposed to consider played out. A governess in a cultivated family, that would treat her kindly and give her £80 to £100 a year, plus board and lodging, was not at all a person to condole with. She expressed sympathy with the Kindergarten system, although the existence of a large Kindergarten near the school rendered it unnecessary to have such a junior department at Edgbaston. Of physical exercises I found Miss Cooper a strong advocate.

" We have a large garden," she said, " and were, I believe, among the first to introduce cricket, but if we had no garden it would be equally possible to obtain exercise indoors. A room can always be fitted up with gymnastic appliances without detriment to its convenience for other purposes. I do not advise violent gymnastic exercises for growing girls. Personally I incline to a modification of the Swedish system, with the introduction of music. But," she added, " play requires to be taught as much as work. One of my first discoveries at Edgbaston," she said with a smile, " was that a headmistress must also be a playmistress."

Recognising with reluctance that I ought not to tarry longer, I asked myself was it possible I had once thought education— how shall I say it?—not fascinating. I perceived that there are educationalists and—others.

MEDICINE.

AN EMINENT LADY DOCTOR.

THE MODESTY OF THE MEDICAL PROFESSION compels me to be mysterious. Fain would I specify with far more precision than the title "An Eminent Lady Doctor" affords, the authority whose views upon her profession I lately solicited, but I am bound by a compact to respect the speaker's desire for anonymity. "Name no names" is the unwritten maxim of the medical profession, which the best of its members obey to the letter. "Name! Name!" cries the public, "and give us not only the name of the personage, but photographs of himself from infancy upwards, and of all his kinsfolk ; of his house likewise, and back garden, his tables, chairs, and (more or less) cosy corners." And nearly everyone, from premier to peasant, obliges the public. Only the medical profession remains magnificently modest. "Name not our names," it says. And the public therefore respects the profession.

Be pleased then to regard my Eminent Lady Doctor as a representative impersonal voice of the women's side of the profession, and do not try to guess the voice's identity.

A Doctor's Equipment.

Time in the consulting-room, where I found myself, was brief ; I addressed myself, therefore, only to those aspects of the subject which appeared to be most worth regarding at the present time. The financial aspect came first

"How is it," I inquired, "that girls who intend to become doctors, do not seem to grudge spending a considerable capital on training themselves, when other girls think twice (and in the end often unfavourably) of paying a moderate fee to apprentice themselves to some other calling?"

"Ah! but the medical profession cannot be regarded like any other calling," said the doctor, earnestly. "One must be born a doctor, as one is born an artist. Nothing else is of any avail; although, of course, a woman who has the medical gift should also possess some other qualifications—first among these, good health. But to the woman who is born a doctor, success is assured. From the pecuniary point of view there is scarcely any other profession that offers a woman at all so generous a reward."

"Nevertheless," I said, "the expenditure of time and money at the outset is considerable, is it not? I suppose a student cannot find time to earn any money during her years of studentship?"

"No, certainly not. Her medical studies will occupy all her time, and now, as you know, five years are required for the London degree."

I ventured to ask the doctor at what amount approximately she would estimate the capital that a girl should spend on her training. "The cost varies" replied my hostess. "The training in Ireland is the most expensive. But it would perhaps be fairer to estimate from the charges of the London School of Medicine for Women. Here the total fees come to £200. Add to that the cost of living for five years, and I should say that £1000 would be about sufficient. But I consider that any young woman would do well to provide herself—either out of this sum, or in addition to it—with the wherewithal to live for a year or two after she has taken her degree. It is quite impossible that she should jump immediately into a lucrative practice. And it is just for want of some means in hand that women rush off to India to take the first post, however small the pay, that offers."

OPENINGS FOR WOMEN DOCTORS.

"But, do you think," I rejoined, "that there are still good openings for women at home?" "Yes, decidedly," she answered cheerfully, "and before long there will be more. My own opinion is that women might be largely employed as assistants to men physicians. A few are so employed already, and are doing well: then, of course, there are official posts to be filled in hospitals. For instance, the Temperance and Homœopathic Hospitals each has a lady on the staff. In lunatic asylums and in infirmaries, too, women might most suitably attend the female patients."

A Special or a Family Practice.

I inquired whether women specialised to any considerable extent—whether, for instance, they were making any peculiar study of the nervous diseases which are the maladies of our age.

The doctor thought not, but she pointed out that women's diseases were naturally the subject to which women practitioners directed their chief attention. She inclined, however, to think that women could do remarkably well in an ordinary family practice.

"It is an arrangement," she observed, "that comes about naturally. The mother of the family consults the woman doctor about herself and her children, and in a short time it becomes convenient to call in the lady whenever there is illness in the family. I do not consider, however, that it is easy for a family to employ a man for some members and a woman for others. Where there is a lady at the head of the house I see no difficulty in prescribing when necessary for the husband or sons."

Perhaps, however, in repeating what the doctor said on this subject, I should do well to remind my readers that the speaker has achieved her high position by many years of experience, and that the course which could be pursued by her with absolute appropriateness would perhaps be modified in the case of a quite young woman. The same distinction that a patient makes between the trusted family physician and the young untried man exists in the case of women doctors, and deserves to be fairly recognised.

Women Doctors' Dispensaries.

Then our talk came, I forget how, to the subject of dispensaries, and my interlocutor spoke with appreciation of the good work that is done, for instance, by Miss McCall, who manages the dispensary and maternity charity at Clapham. A dispensary, however, is a benevolent luxury that only a woman in large practice can afford herself.

"Women of the working class," said the doctor, "have scarcely any money at their disposal. At my own dispensary we charge each woman fourpence a month, and threepence for each child up to the number of three; any other children in the family are doctored gratis. Medicine is sold at twopence a bottle. The dispensary, as you may suppose, does not pay its doctor; indeed, it does not support itself."

How the Public Regard Women Doctors.

Finally, I asked whether women doctors had now quite established themselves in public confidence. Had patients quite got over the idea that they were risking their health magnanimously to oblige a fellow-woman? The doctor laughed genially. "Oh! yes," said she; "I think all that feeling has quite passed away. Indeed, women as physicians are treated with absolute confidence. But with regard to women surgeons, a slight hesitation is still shown. Patients will allow a woman to diagnose the most complicated cases; but, if there is ever so small an operation to be performed, they would rather employ a man to carry out her directions. There is a reason for this scepticism. Hitherto women have enjoyed very little surgical practice; but the facilities afforded by the Hospital for Women, and, I trust, in the future, by many other hospitals, will give women the necessary experience and remove just this one last vestige of prejudice."

With these words of encouragement in my ears, I left to make room for the patients waiting to be ushered into the kindly presence of a woman doctor as sympathetic and wise as she is eminent.

DENTISTRY.

MRS. BOSWELL.

TO BE OR NOT TO BE—a dentist is a question with which the mind of not many an English maiden is distraught. Some explanation for this attitude of indifference towards dentistry should be suggested, I am aware, for the reader never expects to be offered a dry fact without some sauce of explanation, however insufficient. And I dare say that were my explanatory offering to take the form of the statement that the College of Surgeons' Examination Board refuses to permit women to go through the examination for the L.D.S. qualification, I should be held to have made the situation sufficiently intelligible. But, unluckily, the explanation does not satisfy me, for do I not recollect that there was once a time when it was impossible that women should be doctors? The doctors, *i.e.*, the men doctors, would not allow it. Where are those doctors and their impossibility now? For when an irresistible Force, namely, Woman, encounters an immovable Body, namely, Man, that Body must either think better of its immobility or prepare to be pulverised. Or, in the language of the vulgar, "When a woman will, she will, you may depend on't." In the case of dentistry she simply has not willed, and has not troubled to test her powers of irresistibility.

Westward across the water professional assemblages of men, it is understood, enjoy fewer of the immovable Body's attributes than they do in this country, whilst women are even more conspicuously an irresistible Force. People in America do not occupy themselves in opposing forces : on the whole, they find it more inspiriting to row down a stream than up it. The American man likes to move on as rapidly as possible himself, and to see the irresistible sex moving too. But the extraordinary thing is, he does not mind seeing the irresistible ones

(From a photograph by Messrs. Elliot and Fry, Baker-street.)

moving in the direction of his own particular "claim."' For instance, if there is one claim more than another that the American has annexed and cultivated with brilliant results, it is dentistry. He has rescued countless teeth from the extracting pincers; he has devised a method which might be termed filling without thrilling, and altogether has invested the dental chair with a halo of mercy it knew not before. Yet this wonderful man (the American man really sometimes seems too good to live!) does not mind American women being dentists too. And dentists accordingly many American women are—so many as to supply the United States, and to leave some over for European needs. In Germany, women dentists, some of whom are Germans with American qualifications, are tolerably numerous. In England there are only two or three, one of them being Mrs. Boswell.

The Delights of Dentistry.

Mrs. Boswell is both a dentist and the wife of a dentist, consequently the inscription "Dr. Boswell" on a doorplate, in the region of doorplates that surrounds Cavendish-square, serves a double purpose. At the same time, the visitor sets foot with a certain degree of anxiety in a house where there are two dental chambers of horrors, and, despite the knowledge of the mitigated methods of America, my spirits certainly rose on finding myself in a cheerful drawing-room, where lurked neither the tray of appalling crochet-hooks, nor the treadle-grinding monster with its whirligig of pain. Even so amiable and gentle a dentist as Mrs. Boswell appears more amiable in the drawing-room, and the visitor is undoubtedly seen to better advantage than in the operating room, where the appearance of one and all must be singularly devoid of personal charm.

One of the chief delights of dentistry it has always seemed to me is the conversational—or rather controversial—advantage that the dentist enjoys over the patient. Under the handicapping conditions of dental procedure, the victim is compelled to listen with apparent acquiescence to the expression of opinions which he could demolish on the instant were he permitted to exercise the time-honoured right of free speech. I have sometimes thought, therefore, that this prerogative of addressing to persons arguments which might otherwise be unheeded or rebutted, and of saying whatever one might be disposed to say at fullest length, would almost reconcile one to the necessity of inflicting some physical pain at the same time. But this, of course, is an unprofessional view.

Dentistry, as I soon learnt from Mrs. Boswell, has fascinations all its own for the born dentist. I asked Mrs. Boswell what drew her to this work.

"I was always fond of dentistry," she answered. "I was brought up in it, for my father was a dentist, and as a girl I was constantly trying experiments, and I read all the dental literature I could find."

"And you were trained "—"At Michigan University. In America, you must know, it is necessary to take a three years' course of study at the dental and medical schools, and of practical work at the hospital. Of couse a preliminary examination is required before entering, and a year must be spent as pupil to a dentist."

DENTAL TRAINING IN ENGLAND.

"How," I inquired, "do the American regulations compare with the English?" "Here," said Mrs. Boswell, "the professional education of a dental student consists of apprenticeship in mechanical dentistry for not less than three years. In addition, the student must attend a dental hospital and school for two years and a general hospital and medical school for eighteen months. These two latter requirements—the attendance at the general and dental hospitals—can be fulfilled contemporaneously. I ought to say besides that the student must have passed some preliminary examination, such as the London Matriculation or the Oxford or Cambridge Higher Local, providing that the subjects of Algebra, Euclid, Latin, and another language be included."

" In the matter of expense, I suppose dentistry has the advantage over medicine." "You mean a dentist's training is cheaper than a doctor's? Well, I hardly think so. The premium for apprenticeship to a dentist is usually between £80 and £300, but is often more, the amount depending on the conditions made about time, the extent of the dentist's practice, and so forth. Hospital fees come to about £100; there are also little extras for dissections, chemistry, &c. Instruments would cost, say £30 to begin with, and as much more as could be afforded later. So you see," said Mrs. Boswell, smiling, " it takes both time and money to make a dentist."

" And when this long, expensive course is finished, an English-woman cannot practise, I suppose?" " No, she must wait until the College of Surgeons will allow her to take her ' L.D.S.,' which they have not done yet."

Overcoming Prejudice.

In a country so unfamiliar with the woman dentist, it appeared to me that Mrs. Boswell must have had some considerable amount of prejudice to conquer at the start. With regard to any achieve-ment of this kind, however, she was very modest, and laid stress on the advantage it had been to her to have her husband's help. " People may have hesitated a little at first," she explained, " but finding, I suppose, that I was sympathetic and gentle, and achieved good results, they recommended me to their friends. And now I have a great many patients who declare they would go to nobody else. I always bestow great care on my operations, and so give very little pain, generally none at all. A good many nervous women come to me, and children, too, form a large part of my practice. Mothers appreciate more now than formerly the im-portance of having children's first teeth attended to, if irregularity is to be prevented later and the shape of the mouth maintained. But schoolgirls and schoolboys, I think, are my favourite patients; they are so plucky."

Mrs. Boswell's devotion to her profession does not blind her to its drawbacks. " Dentistry is not healthy work," she said, "and no woman who is not thoroughly robust should think of undertaking it. The standing, the stooping, and the nervous strain are all injurious to health. True, at the end of the day one is free to go out, but often by that time one is altogether too tired to take exercise. I am bound to acknowledge, by my own experience, that dentistry is mentally and physically most wearing. I ought to say further, that a woman must possess some mechanical ingenuity to make a success."

Just as I was leaving, Mrs. Boswell threw open a door and revealed the " chamber of horrors." There stood the deceptively comfortable-looking red velvet chair and all the familiar apparatus, the whirligig of pain not excluded. The appearance of the room was harmonious and tranquil, and the gentle manner of Mrs. Boswell most soothing; but I confess I was not sorry to turn away from a scene fraught with so many painful emotions.

NURSING.

MRS. BEDFORD FENWICK.

IN the history of all human affairs there are moments of sudden progress and unexpected activity, which are followed by long periods of uneventful quietude, of silence, it may be perchance of retrogression. It is so in the case of the professions in which men and women engage. There are times when the members of a profession are simply doing their duty—as their predecessors have understood it—in a jog-trot way, consoling themselves with a somewhat cheerless "Virtue is its own reward" philosophy. And there come moments, again, when the members—or rather the younger ones among them—are suddenly inspired with ideas which make their work a delight as well as a duty, and with aspirations for the glory of their profession which send them forth gaily to encounter and to conquer opposition.

A Revolution in the Hospitals.

Amongst the professions which are in the throes of renaissance, the nursing profession is at the present moment a notable example. Rumours of its internal warfare, and the sound of its battle-cries —registration and anti-registration—have reached the ears of the public. A good many outsiders find themselves, nevertheless, in the position of Southey's old Kaspar :

> But what they fought each other for
> I could not well make out.

The ideas of the younger generation in the nursing world are not, however, difficult to understand, or at least it is the fault of the auditor if the matter, as explained by Mrs. Bedford Fenwick, is not clearly intelligible.

Mrs. Fenwick's Nursing Career.

Mrs. Bedford Fenwick speaks with authority upon nursing matters, for she has climbed the professional ladder to its topmost rung, beginning as a probationer in the Children's Hospital at Nottingham, proceeding thence to the Manchester Royal Infirmary. In due course she received promotion, and was offered the post of sister at the London Hospital, and in eighteen months from her arrival in the metropolis she was appointed (in 1881) to be matron of St. Bartholomew's. Her marriage with Dr. Bedford Fenwick some six years later led to her abandonment of hospital work, but it has given her more leisure than she could otherwise have had to devote to the consideration of nursing politics. For example, from her emanated the idea of the British Nurses' Association, and she took the chief part in its organisation and working for the first few years of its existence, until, in fact, it had attained success by being incorporated by Royal Charter. Mrs. Fenwick was selected to organise the British Nursing Section at the Chicago Exhibition, and the Report to Congress gave special praise to the success which she achieved. She was awarded the Helena Gold Medal of Merit for Nurses, in acknowledgment of her work for and in her profession. In short, from all her past work and from her present position as editor of the *Nursing Record*, she is recognised as a representative leader of the nursing world. Mrs. Fenwick now inhabits a comfortable house in the medical quarter, and it was there that I found her one day, very busily engaged in the work of her journal, but very willing to give me the information for which I wished on various matters.

"And now, Mrs. Fenwick," I said, "I want you kindly to tell me how this demand for registration came about."

The Sweating of Private Nurses.

"That would be a long story," said Mrs. Fenwick. "I suppose the history of the movement dates back pretty nearly to the time, some twenty or five-and-twenty years ago, when educated ladies were first introduced into hospitals, instead of the untrained and often incapable women of the charwoman class who were formerly employed. Ladies effected great and valuable improvements in the methods of nursing, but the authorities at first hardly knew how to treat them, and expected them to do the menial work which their predecessors had performed. Then came the introduction of ward-maids, and this grievance was redressed. But somehow," she continued, "in our nursing world we have no sooner removed one abuse than another has arisen. We had, for instance, no sooner swept the hospitals of our incapable and oft-times drunken Sairey Gamps, and had put the nursing of our hospitals upon the best possible footing, than an unexpected trouble occurred.

" The hospital authorities began, in short, to perceive that they possessed in their lady nurses an unexpected source of revenue. The public outside the hospitals began to ask for trained nurses. At first, no doubt, the public got what it asked for, but gradually some few institutions slipped into the habit of sending out only half trained nurses to a public which did not know the difference : the temptation was a pecuniary one, and was certainly strong. A nurse at the end of her first year's training will be receiving a nominal salary of from £12 to £16. But let her be sent into private families as a ' fully trained ' nurse, and she is forthwith earning for her employers two guineas a week. Everybody is defrauded by such a system—the private employer who pays at a critical moment for the services of a competent person and does not get them, and the nurse, who is both defrauded of a large sum of money which she has earned and of the training which she entered the hospital on the understanding she should receive. Nor is this all. Ultimately the hospital patients suffer also from this dishonest system. Often the supply of nurses from the Private Nursing Home runs short, and then nurses are taken out of the wards to send to private houses. You may suppose what dis-organisation of hospital management can ensue from such a system."

THE FAIR SYSTEM.

"I should like to know, Mrs. Fenwick," I asked at this point, " what would be in your estimation a fair system of remuneration for private nurses—fair, I mean, to all parties ? "

"The system which prevails at some of the best private institu-tions, is, I think, a good one. The nurses are there paid a salary of £30, and 25 per cent. on their earnings. This means generally about £50, with board, lodging, and travelling expenses found.

But no nurse should be allowed to take private nursing cases at all who has not had three years' hospital training. There are several hospitals I could name—in particular, St. Bartholomew's and the Middlesex—where these conditions are rigidly observed. But these are splendid exceptions to the rule in force at some other metropolitan and provincial hospitals.

"Still the system which is now finding such public favour is the most fair system of all. It is exemplified in the Registered Nurses' Society, of 269, Regent-street, which I started, and of which I am the hon. superintendent. It is managed by an honorary committee of medical men and nurses. The members are carefully picked nurses, each one of whom has had at least three years' hospital training, and has been registered by the Royal British Nurses' Association, after the most careful inquiry into her personal character and professional work. The society sends out these nurses to the public, and they receive their full earnings, less a commission of $7\frac{1}{2}$ per cent. to defray the office expenses. This society has been a great success because the public know now where to secure the best possible nurses, and the nurses on their part are fairly paid for their work. Such co-operations of nurses will, I believe, in the future be the system by which the best class of women will take up private nursing."

What Registration will Secure.

" Registration will insure a nurse reaching a certain standard of efficiency and experience before she is allowed to engage in private nursing practice. If the nurse's name is on the register, the doctor who recommends her, and the family who engage her, will know that that nurse has had three years' hospital training, and that she has satisfied the authorities in her profession of her efficiency."

"Well, but Mrs. Fenwick, we hear the objection urged that nurses who are upon the register may have the requisite knowledge, but may lack the highest practical or moral qualities. How do you meet this ? I suppose you would say that the Medical Register does not guarantee that every man on its books is strictly sober, of high moral character, and the rest; but it does guarantee a certain standard of ability and knowledge."

" Precisely ; and, moreover," continued Mrs. Fenwick, " we

must look to the matrons of hospitals to discourage nurses from completing their course of training if they are manifestly unsuited for the profession. But what I do feel is that registration will immensely raise the self-respect of nurses by raising their profession in the eyes of others."

THE ORGANISATION OF THE R.B.N.A.

The comparison between the nursing and the medical professions led me to advance a criticism—or at least an inquiry—of my own. I asked, " Why, if the nursing profession were to manage its own affairs, should a considerable number of medical men serve upon its council? would it not seem a strange thing if nurses undertook to advise doctors upon the management of their professional affairs? "

Mrs. Fenwick received this objection with much courtesy, but I found her quite prepared to meet it. She showed me that I was too logical in treating nurses and doctors alike. The doctor was an independent personage, but the nurse depended upon the doctor, and should at all times be his subordinate. Moreover, the help of the doctors had been of great practical value to the association. Mrs. Fenwick then described to me how the association manages its affairs. The entire association meets annually, and elects its council by ballot, the council consisting of 100 doctors, 100 matrons, and 100 sisters and nurses. This council, in its turn, elects the executive committee, which comprises nearly an equal number of doctors and matrons, with one hospital sister. Both on the General Council and the Executive Committee there are a certain number of *ex-officio* members who are the matrons of large hospitals, who sit on the governing bodies of the association by virtue of their public positions, and who therefore represent their training schools. The hospitals like this, because it recognises their right to a voice in the management of the association, and the nurses especially approve of the leaders of their profession being permanent members of the Council and Committee. Finally, the interest these ladies have thus taken in the association has really been the chief reason for the rapid success it has achieved. The association can claim with perfect justice that its whole organisation is, therefore, strictly representative.

Women as Hospital Governors.

The interviewer who has been told a great deal always wants to know more. Consequently I tried to elicit something further from the ex-hospital matron. " Were hospitals satisfactorily governed at present ?"

No; Mrs. Fenwick thought the whole system, or want of system, most unsatisfactory. Any rich, well-meaning gentleman, even if he knew nothing about the management of hospitals, could, on payment of a certain sum of money, become a life governor. The result of this plan was that the average governing body was entirely in the hands of its officials, who could manage the whole nursing institution. " At the same time," said Mrs. Fenwick, " I believe it is very important to keep the management of hospitals in the hands of laymen. I dislike extremely all that tends towards institutionalism or the growth of a close corporation. When I think about this subject, I am often reminded of the ancient Hospital of the Knights Templar, where it was the rule that a stream of clear water should run through every ward. It is just such a stream," she added, speaking with intensity, " the wholesome stream of public opinion, that we need to flow through our hospitals. But the opinion must be educated. And that is why I wish so much to see more women upon hospital committees. Women have the leisure to give to the study of hospital management which the average man of business lacks, and if we could encourage some women to do for hospitals what Miss Louisa Twining has done for workhouses, many petty abuses would be swept away."

The Future of Nursing.

With regard to the future of the nursing profession, Mrs. Fenwick is very clear. She is much pleased that the R.B.N.A. has gained its Royal Charter, and she regards that as the best proof of the success and public utility of the association. She wishes to have an International Nursing Congress to settle the foundation principles of a uniform education for nurses, and then to have an Act passed for a council to control the nursing profession of the future. She firmly believes she is destined to live to see the International Nursing Congress and the Act of Parliament, and to take her share in bringing both to pass.

MISS DE PLEDGE.

(From a photograph by Pragnell and Co., Sloane-street.)

INFIRMARY NURSING.

MISS DE PLEDGE

(MATRON OF THE CHELSEA INFIRMARY).

THE best infirmary nursing at the present time is in all
essentials hospital nursing. The remark sounds painfully
trite, but it is in reality the expression of a quite recent fact. To
consider that a poor man and a pauper should be tended when ill
with equal care is one of the most modern of opinions, which,
even if held, is not, I believe, yet practised everywhere. My
memory, and that doubtless of many of you who read, recalls
with no effort whatever the picture of a cold blank colourless
ward, furnished merely with a double row of beds in which old
people lay facing each other, often enduring atrocious sufferings
which the decrepit and sometimes imbecile crones, their nominal
sick attendants, could not attempt to relieve. Nothing in life
could more nearly resemble death than the condition of these
miserable beings, waiting through months and years of pain in
beds which were at once their prison and their grave till the last
order of release should come.

If we wish to appreciate the reform that has been effected in
Poor Law Infirmary administration—and it is well that we should
so wish, seeing that reform has been almost entirely accomplished
by women—we must think of the deplorable system now passing
away. If, with those thoughts in mind, we enter the Chelsea
Infirmary we shall not consider it a matter of course that this
institution should be as perfectly organised as the best of hospitals,
that the wards should be bright, airy, tastefully decorated ; that
trained nurses with cultivated minds and kindly hearts should
wait upon the patients, and that the matron should be a lady of

the highest competence in the nursing profession. Least of all is this last and highest advantage to be taken for granted, since the infirmaries are still many where the matron has no knowledge of nursing.

THE ADVANTAGES AND DRAWBACKS OF INFIRMARY NURSING.

But however much we may deplore the fact that workhouse infirmary patients should not have been, nor be yet generally, so efficiently treated as patients in a hospital, it would be uncandid to pretend that the cases of the two classes of sufferers are on all fours. The hospital patient is assumed to be a person curable, and rapidly curable, by medical treatment and skilful nursing But (leaving the children out of account) the average infirmary patient is an aged, worn-out being, upon whom no nursing miracle can be performed. His path down hill may be made smoother and less grievous to him, but that is about all.

Can the infirmaries, then, succeed in attracting the best nurses? This was the question I had in mind when I called on Miss De Pledge, and I put it to her at an early period in our chat. "I never," said the matron, "have the least difficulty in getting nurses or probationers, and the staff here will compare favourably with that of any institution in London." ("Yes," thought I, "and if all matrons were Miss De Pledges, infirmary nursing would be the most popular of pursuits.") "Infirmary nursing, as a whole," she continued, "does not afford the same attractions as hospital nursing. Infirmaries have no medical schools attached to them, and there is a larger number proportionately of chronic and bedridden cases. Those infirmaries, too, which are without a trained matron lack the first requisite for the formation of a nursing school. On the other hand, there are abundant opportunities for studying the everyday ailments and troubles of the poor. We see cases, for instance, of pneumonia and bronchitis that are rarely met with in hospitals. The patients are often in a shocking state of debility, consequent on drink, poverty, and neglect. No, I am glad to say the prejudice against infirmary nursing is disappearing; but much work remains to be done in this department, and I hope that in the future the tendency of poor law administration may be to improve and enlarge our infirmaries."

System of Training.

Miss De Pledge is such an active member of the Royal British Nurses' Association that I felt sure nothing less than the regulation three years' training for nurses would content her. In this I was right, for she told me that although one year was the period of probationership, nurses would be expected to remain in the Infirmary for another couple of years if there were any post vacant for them. The probationer on becoming a staff nurse receives a salary of £18 a year, plus the sum of £3 10s. for "beer money." "That is one of the little peculiarities of the Poor Law," Miss De Pledge explained, "and I need scarcely say our nurses generally prefer the money to the beer." "From staff nurses I suppose they rise to become sisters?" I inquired. "Not sisters," corrected Miss De Pledge, "we have no such title in this infirmary; charge nurses we call them."

"What are the chances of promotion for nurses when they leave you?" "I should say they were very good," was the reply. "Nurses trained here have seldom any difficulty in obtaining posts. They generally go to some other infirmary either in the capacity of charge nurse or of night superintendent, The latter is the higher post, and carries with it a salary of from £30 to £40."

With the inquirer's avidity for details, I asked Miss De Pledge to tell me how the work of the infirmary was organised, and she kindly responded by saying that the building contains 400 beds, thirty-four to thirty-eight in each ward, and forty-three cots in the children's ward—eleven wards in all. One charge nurse superintends the children's ward. "It is necessarily," said the matron, "a very busy ward, for we get quite young infants, from two or three days old and upwards, who want constant attention." The five other charge nurses take two wards apiece. Then to each ward there is an allowance of a staff nurse and a probationer

Students of Sanitary Science.

"Besides probationers, do you not now take pupils from the National Health Society?"—"Yes, for the last two years we have been receiving pupils who wish to qualify themselves by obtaining a knowledge of nursing to become lecturers on hygienic subjects for the County Councils. These pupils—there are generally from four to six of them—come here for six months training, for which they pay at the rate of 15s. per week. They do not live under this roof, and at the end of their short training are, of course, in no sense to be considered as nurses; but the general experience in the treatment of the sick which they can gain here is, no doubt, of the utmost value to them, whether they become lecturers or take other posts."

"And now that sanitary inspectorships are being freely opened to women," I interposed, "the opportunities you offer must be more than ever valuable." "Yes; I hope that the infirmary may offer a valuable field of experience to future inspectors. I need not remind you that the Factory inspector, Miss Deane, and Miss Squire, the Sanitary inspector, were formerly pupils of ours. I consider that the system has been most successful in every way."

How Miss De Pledge became Matron.

At this moment the introduction of tea, and with it some delicate girdle cakes of a kind unknown to Londoners, led us to talk of the North country, and I learned that my hostess (though, doubtless, her family is of Huguenot origin) had spent her early life in the Weardale district of Durham, where her father was rector of a parish. Her mother, she added, was one of the well-known Northumberland family of Fenwicks. To leave her home and all its ties had not been achieved without difficulty; but an irresistible desire for a nurse's life drew her to St. Bartholomew's, where she worked for some years very happily under the admirable matronship of the lady who is now Mrs. Bedford Fenwick. Then came an appointment to be night superintendent at the Chelsea Infirmary, followed, after a few months, by a call to the matron's post.

To this simple sounding history of success my own observation easily supplied the explanation as, with the matron's escort, I went round the wards and saw the admirable order and the cheerfulness that everywhere prevailed. "Miss De Pledge is tremendously strict, but she is always kind," somebody who had worked under her told me not long since. I saw the truth of these words on the one hand in the perfect discipline which makes the wheels of this great establishment move without hitch; for not only the wards, but the big kitchen, and a laundry, where 6000 articles are washed weekly, are under Miss De Pledge's direct survey. On the other hand, I noted how, as we lingered in the children's ward, the tiny creatures ran to their kind matron, clinging round her, and showing her their toys with that unconstrained simple affection which is a finer compliment than any that adult human beings can pay to each other.

But I am concluding and forgetting to mention one of the most important inmates—Miss De Pledge's Irish terrier, Randolph, whose portrait is here given with that of his mistress. But for his timely warning a fire, which once broke out in the matron's suite of rooms, might have been undetected till too late. No; the queen of the infirmary's most faithful subject deserves something better than the last word.

SCHOOL BOARD WORK.

MRS. HOMAN, M.L.S.B.

NOT EVERY WOMAN grasps the fact that, be she married, widowed, or single, propertied or the reverse, she is equally eligible to serve as a member of those important public bodies, the School Boards, if the voters are pleased to have her. That women are wanted I had no doubt prior to my visit to Mrs. Homan, but the need was made more urgent to me by the talk which I enjoyed with that most able and conscientious London School Board member.

Mrs. Homan s time is so entirely devoted to her work that it was with difficulty a half-hour was spared for me ; therefore no moments were lost before proceeding to business.

ADVICE TO WOULD-BE CANDIDATES.

" The School Boards would be the better for more women ; may I assume ? " said I, wishing to have the best authority for the statement. " Yes, by all means," said Mrs. Homan, " we sadly want women. There are many reasons why the London School Board wants them, but one reason is patent to everybody—I mean the fact that there are nearly twice as many women teachers as men. The actual numbers are 5188 mistresses and 2606 masters ; the women teaching both girls and infants, the masters only the boys. In discussing the qualifications of women for the School Board I should be inclined to give a preference, other things equal, to married women, because there are many matters which the mistresses and parents would more readily confide to a married than to an unmarried lady. But the qualification to which I attach the most importance is a general interest in education. On the Board recently there have been beside Miss Davenport-

MRS. HOMAN, M.L.S.B.

Hill, Miss Eve, and Mr. Lyulph Stanley, very few members who were primarily educationalists. And a third requirement is robust health."

SOME POINTS ABOUT THE ELECTION.

" And, granted all or either of these qualifications, Mrs. Homan, how is the willing candidate to make known her willingness to those whom it may concern ? "

" Usually the best plan would be for the candidate to put herself into relations with one of the political societies. In London, on the side to which I belong, the body to apply to is the Progressive School Board Council. The candidate also should endeavour to form a committee, consisting of persons representing as many interests as possible, to support her. Then she issues her address, and the campaign begins."

" Is an election a very expensive affair ? "

"It may be estimated, I think, to cost from £60 to £80. Candidates are expected, of course, to defray the cost themselves; at the same time, if want of means is a difficulty, and the candidate is considered specially desirable, the political organisation will sometimes supply the funds."

LIVING LABORIOUS DAYS.

"Robust health, you were saying, is a *sine quâ non.*" Mrs. Homan bore traces of exhaustion which were not apparent when I made her acquaintance three years ago. " I suppose it is those sittings we read about, beginning somewhere about midday, and ending somewhere about midnight, that are so trying ? " " Oh, I am thankful to say those trials of strength are rare occurrences. They only happen when we get upon the religious question. No ; the actual Thursday Board Meeting is almost the least fatiguing part of the week's routine."

" But do you mean that the School Board absorbs the entire week ? " " I reckon to give five whole days to it," she replied. And then I asked Mrs. Homan to sketch the programme of the week's work, which she kindly did. But I regret to say that I lost pace with the bewildering recital through wondering how Mrs. Homan fitted lunch in on one day, and where the harmless necessary tea was placed on another; and I recognised too late

E

that there are neither intervals for refreshment nor for thinking about it in the programme of a conscientious member of the Board. I learned, however, that it is the five Grand Committees which, with their sub-committees, absorb most of the time. Mrs. Homan contended that there should be at least one lady on each of these grand committees, namely, School Management, Works, Finance (with its sub-committee for stores, such as cooking and needlework materials), School Accommodation and Attendance, and Industrial Schools. On several of these departments Mrs. Homan offered interesting suggestions. Referring to the domestic subjects, she spoke of the success of the housewifery centre at Hammersmith, and mentioned a plan that she would like to see carried out for teaching more of the practice and less of the theory of housewifery, and for systematising the teaching of domestic subjects, so as to economise time   Speaking of industrial schools, she told me that the Board was obliged to send children to schools sometimes as far distant as Bath, which members of the Board felt it incumbent on them to visit, and that it would be a great advantage that the Board should have an industrial school of its own. I also found that Mrs. Homan took an active interest in those special schools for the deficient under the direction of Mrs. Burgwin, which are described elsewhere in this volume. "These schools," said Mrs. Homan, "have been a great help to us in unearthing cases that we have sent to Darenth and else-where—children kept at home on account of their deficiencies, whom we should not have discovered otherwise. From my own observation I can testify to the marked improvement in the children who have been some time in the special schools."

But the work of all these committees (which entails endless peregrinations to schools and centres), though more than sufficient to dispel *ennui*, does not exhaust the lengthy programme, for every member is responsible to the district that elects him or her. Mrs. Homan, for instance, was elected by the Tower Hamlets; consequently, once a month she attends the divisional meeting of the members for that district. After the meeting, if not obliged to attend a committee at the Board offices, she proceeds to visit one or more of the group of schools which each member has to look after. " We are referred to about all sorts of little matters by our particular schools. A teacher, for instance, must let me know if she is ill and unable to attend; and only the other day I was asked to give leave for a display of bunting in honour of a visit to the neighbourhood by the Prince of Wales."

"Surely the school managers exist in order to relieve you in these little ways?" "No, they are not authorised to do so at present. I should like, though, to see managers made far more responsible than at present, and allotted definite duties. But no change of the kind can be made till they are more carefully chosen. It is not uncommon to find somebody cheerfully nominating a person as manager and another supporting him, and neither knowing anything really about the qualifications of their applicant."

I inquired tentatively whether this exacting daily round endured throughout the year, and was encouraged on learning that the holidays are planned in a generous spirit—two months in summer, five weeks at Christmas, four at Easter, and, I think, three at Whitsuntide. "But, of course," added Mrs. Homan, "there is plenty that may be done during the holidays; there are schools to visit, individual children to look after, and much else to do." And I did not doubt there was. Country boards, however, it is assumed by Londoners, take things much more easily, having fewer things to take. Let us hope that ladies serving on country boards assent to this cheerful view.

If by this unvarnished tale of school board toil I have scared any timid sister, let me counteract the effect by saying that Mrs. Homan spoke with conviction of the absorbing and increasing interest in her work which would repay a woman for any sacrifice of time and ease she might make in the cause of human helpfulness.

POOR LAW ADMINISTRATION.

MRS. McCALLUM, P.L.G.

IS THE ADMINISTRATION of the Poor Law a profession? Not in one sense. A Poor Law Guardian draws no income from her or his labour; in many cases it might be said an income is drawn from her or him. Yet in a broader sense this and all other departments of public work ought to be regarded as professions. The Poor Law Guardian must be imbued with the professional, as distinguished from the amateur spirit; for work that is done in the professional spirit is the only kind that wears, and that is as good in the inconspicuous places as in those that catch the eye of everybody. For this reason I reckon the administration of the Poor Law among the professions, and so, I believe, would Mrs. McCallum, as may presently be inferred.

Mrs. McCallum obtained her initiation into the science of philanthropy as a member of the Charity Organisation Society and as a School Manager. She is now (1894) in her third term of office as a member of the Chelsea Board of Guardians, and the circumstance of her appointment as the only lady judge of the Charities department at the World's Fair to represent this country should give the Chelsea electors cause for pride in their choice. Mrs. McCallum's opinions upon Poor Law administration are, therefore, of peculiar interest, seeing that they are drawn from personal observation over an unusually wide area.

SCIENTIFIC PHILANTHROPY.

Mrs. McCallum is no sentimentalist; that I discovered as soon as I had propounded the inevitable question about outdoor relief. She met my question by another.

" Have you ever studied the conditions of pauperism in this

country before the Poor Law of 1834 was passed? If so, you will not wish to increase the amount of outdoor relief."

"But what about the cases that one reads of almost every day, of people dying of starvation rather than go into the workhouse?" Mrs. McCallum astonished me by her reply, "It is just these people who frequently are in receipt of out-door relief. Of course," she continued, "drunkenness and other faults are often at the bottom of their misfortunes. But in nine cases out of ten, the guardians get the blame instead of the real culprits. For instance, you may remember reading the case some time ago of a man who deserted his family because his wife was a drunkard, and the children were starved in consequence Great indignation was expressed against the guardians for not coming to the assistance of the children; but I waited in vain for anyone to point out that the man was to blame for leaving his children at the mercy of their mother."

"Possibly," I suggested, "if you are not in favour of the distribution of relief, you would advocate that the workhouses should be made more comfortable?"

"I think many of them are too comfortable already," Mrs. McCallum replied.

"Would not you wish to make the lives of the old people a little less dull than they are present?"

"Do you think," asked the Lady Guardian in return, "that dulness belongs entirely to their surroundings, or partly to the incapacity and indifference of old age? I am in favour, however, of doing whatever can be done for the really deserving old people, who are, I think, chiefly women. That the old couples should be allowed to live together is also quite proper; but," she added, with a smile, "they do not so often wish to live together as you might suppose. What we do need, in short, is a better system of classification; but in an old building, such as the Chelsea Workhouse, this is impossible. We should be obliged to erect a new building, and the ratepayers would grumble terribly at such an expense."

Charity and Politics in America.

When our talk turned presently to the position of affairs in the States, Mrs. McCallum told me that she thought the class of "loafers" was more successfully limited in America than here, and that, with no charitable provision for its support, its existence was naturally curtailed. The Charity Organisation Society, she told me further, was a strong force in the States.

TECHNICAL TRAINING FOR PAUPER CHILDREN.

I then inquired whether the Americans were more successful than ourselves in giving a technical training to pauper children. "I have not," was the reply, "visited Industrial Schools enough to be able to institute a comparison, but, judging by the exhibits at the World's Fair, I should say that there is a better attempt at education as distinguished from mere cram. We all know the value of manual training as a means of developing accuracy of hand and eye, as well as of patience and thoroughness. The Americans endeavour to give this training through such systems as the Slöyd, whereas people in England are apt to think that work in a tailor's or bootmaker's school shop is as good, viewing the matter from the commercial standpoint rather than the educational. I was much impressed with a visit I paid to the Lyman-street School of Boston. The school is in the country, and the boys are encouraged to write weather reports, to grow seeds in their rooms, and to watch and describe the plants. They are taught wood-carving as well as Slöyd. All their studies are directed towards the development of their intelligence and taste."

ARE MORE WOMEN GUARDIANS WANTED?

I then propounded a final question in full expectation of an affirmative reply. "You are," I said, "no doubt pleased at the lowering of the rate-paying qualification, which will now enable many women to become guardians who were formerly ineligible?" But Mrs. McCullum was only affirmative with considerable reservations.

"If you had asked me," she said, "whether I wished to see well-qualified women elected as guardians, my answer would be an unhesitating 'Yes.' But I am not desirous that a woman candidate should be chosen merely because she is a woman. The advent of the untrained and emotional woman into Poor Law administration is much to be feared, for her power for evil will be as great as her power for good. During the last sixty years the flood of pauperism has been to some extent checked, but careless hands may quickly make a fatal breach in a dam that it has taken wit and labour to build; and women are often more ready to act than to think."

VESTRY WORK.

MRS. SHELDON AMOS.

IN THE CAPACITY OF VOTER for a London Vestry, I was favoured shortly before the recent elections with a list of persons whose merits I was asked especially to consider, in view of such humble electoral part as I might play at the polling station. Knowing that a lady had offered herself as candidate for this particular Vestry, I primarily searched the list to find her name. She was not among the chosen. Thinking it possible she had withdrawn from the contest, I wrote to inquire the reason of the omission. The reply I received was to the effect that this candidate's claims were still before the electors, but it was considered that the Vestry would offer no opportunities for work of which a woman could avail herself with profit to the inhabitants of the district.

This answer might prove, by the light of practical experience of women's work on Vestries, to be quite correct. But, in the meantime, since no women had taken part in Vestry work, no such experience had been gained. The reply of the gentleman to whom I had referred appeared, therefore, to be chiefly theoretical. And recollecting the frequency with which a little feminine practice upsets much man-made theory, I recorded my first vote— my readers will, I trust, not think me perverse—for the lady in question. But the average elector, being shy of taking an experimental step, did not rally to the support of the women candidates for the Vestries with the same warmth that he backed up the claims of women to Boards of Guardians, where he knew the merits of the sex from of old. Of the many ladies who stood, but few were chosen, and my particular candidate was not among the fortunate minority. Here and there, however, it happened either that the ladies inspired especial confidence, or that the elector

MRS. SHELDON AMOS.

(Photographed by Fradell and Young, 246, Regent-street, W.)

was a person of enlightenment. Probably both causes were combined in Marylebone. In that parish three ladies, Mrs. Sheldon Amos, the Hon. Miss Carew, and Miss Willoughby were returned.

THE SNOW GRIEVANCE.

It was on a wintry day, when the north wind did blow, and we did have snow—the particular type of day when the mind coldly turns to thoughts of Vestries—that I moved towards Marylebone. To be perfectly fair, there was a little snow even in Marylebone, and even near my bourne, the dwelling of Mrs. Sheldon Amos.

But the feminine broom cannot be expected to sweep everything clean at once; it suffices that it should make an effort so to do. And I had not been many minutes in the presence of Mrs. Sheldon Amos before I discovered that she was far more concerned about the snow grievance than the most grumbling ratepayer could be.

"I should like," said Mrs. Amos, "to see the snow got rid of far more rapidly than it usually is in London. But you must remember that the men for whom the Vestries find such employment as this are often not of the most efficient class. They are generally very poor, often underfed, and, of course it is extremely desirable that they should obtain employment; at the same time, they require a great deal of looking after."

This I was not surprised to hear, and I mentioned that in the domain of a neighbouring Vestry, the nominal sweepers had lately been observed by a lady to be standing shivering in the snow, swinging their arms against their bodies to get warm, when this result might more swiftly have been attained by the exercise in which they were supposed to be engaged. Mrs. Amos laughed. "Yes, they require continual overlooking,"; she rejoined, "And, do you know, I think women could very well be employed as overseers." This innovation found me unprepared, and I am afraid that I smiled.

"But I mean it quite seriously," she continued, "and I said as much lately at the Vestry. However, I am not sanguine enough to expect the suggestion to be carried out immediately."

It was rather too early, I felt, to expect Mrs. Amos to tell me at all the precise kind of services which women could render on Vestries. Indeed, I soon discovered that she was modestly disposed to look upon herself for the present as rather a learner than a teacher of the work upon which she had only for so short a time been engaged.

" What, however," said Mrs. Amos, " I can safely advise is that women, to acquire a knowledge of the local administration in their own district, should attend Vestry meetings from time to time. They would learn much in this way of which they are ignorant at present.   For there is nothing that handicaps women so much in the performance of practical public duties such as these, as the habitual limitation of their lives.   It is so much easier for men than for women to acquire a knowledge of practical outside things. In casual encounters with each other, in the course of ordinary chat, they pick up all kinds of knowledge which never is brought to the ears of women.   Men, indeed, often avoid such subjects in talking to a lady, thinking probably that she will not be interested in them.

" And thus it is that women are very seldom enabled to bring their general principles to the touchstone of practice.   Not that I think these principles need crumble away by the contact.   But it is impossible that they should not be modified at various points in deference to the complex conditions of human life."

BATHS AND WASH-HOUSES.

Recollecting that Marylebone was said to be exercised on the question of baths and wash-houses, and that Mrs. Amos had made a well-considered speech on the subject at a recent Vestry meeting, I asked for some further particulars.   Mrs. Amos then told me that the baths and wash-houses building, which stood at the west end of Maryleborne-road, had lately been condemned and pulled down.   Upon the site it had been proposed to erect a new building for the purpose, at a cost which seemed to many of the Vestry, including herself, extremely heavy.   For several reasons, but chiefly on account of the size of the parish, and the distance which women must carry their clothes, it appeared to her desirable to arrange several small wash-houses in the poorer districts, instead of, or in addition to, the proposed building on the present site.

" I think," she said, " it might be desirable to place the Baths in a central situation, but Wash-houses ought to be distributed over the parish in those localities where they are most needed.   In the first instance I would advocate leasing premises, so that we may see whether they prove to be useful and convenient."

" Are the wash-houses very much used then?" I inquired. "Yes" said Mrs. Amos. " Have you never been in one? The wash-houses in Marylebone, I am told, were always crowded, and many of the women, I am afraid, had to wait a long time for their turn. Now, of course, it is worse; for the Marylebone women are obliged to go to the Paddington and other neighbouring wash-houses, which are a great distance from the homes of many. A large wash-house," she continued, "must inevitably be expensive to build. It requires to be of great solidity on account of the machinery for the steam boilers, hydro-extractors, mangles, &c."

" Cannot the women work the hand-mangles?" I asked. "Yes, no doubt they could. But I am told that these mangles were so often broken through the women trying to force in too many clothes, that the steam mangles were found, in the long run, to be cheaper."

It may be worth while to add that, since this conversation, I visited the baths and wash-houses in Bloomsbury, and I found there that Bradford's wringers were in constant use, and that little complaint was made on the score of injury to the machines by carelessness. On the day of my inspection I found a great crowd and several women waiting, but I was told that it was a day of rather a light attendance, the end of the week being always the busiest time. In the preceding week I was shown a record of 1000 attendances. With regard to the baths, which I found extremely clean and well managed, I was interested to learn that they are used by men in far larger numbers than by women. The disproportion between the sexes, however, seems to diminish somewhat in warm weather, though even then, from a hasty glance at the figures, I could not find that the proportion of women bathers rose to more than a third of the total of men. I merely state these facts, but it would not be difficult to find reasons for them in women's lack of spare time and money.

THE VESTRY AND THE HOME.

Considering only this matter of the baths and wash-houses, it appeared to me there was sufficient refutation of the objection that there was nothing for women to do on Vestries; but Mrs. Amos went on to refer to various other sides of Vestry work which are closely connected with home interests.

For instance, there is the question of providing safeguards against epidemics. The Vestry is about to build a new disinfector and more rooms for receiving infected families while their clothing and rooms are undergoing purification. In the arrangement of these premises it is reasonable to imagine that a shrewd, capable woman could offer serviceable hints; and, to my thinking, what is by no means least valuable to the community at large is that women, by the very responsibility which devolves upon them in such ways as this, will learn to know more of the actual character of their poorer neighbours than they can ever do when they approach the poor in the capacity of irresponsible philanthropists.

One more point touched on in the course of conversation was the collection of dust and house refuse. "There has been some discussion," said Mrs. Amos, "about the manner in which the householder should be notified that the dust-cart is in his vicinity. Would it be sufficient that the dust-man should announce his presence by calling out as he drives along the street, or should the householder be required to put a printed ticket in his window; or should a boy accompany the cart and call at the door of each house? I inclined to the last suggestion, as it seemed to me that there were objections to each of the others, especially in the case of the poor, who cannot always be at home to look out for the cart, nor are their windows generally so conspicuously situated that a printed D. could catch the dust-man's eye. And, although the poor may have less refuse than the rich it is much more necessary that what there is should be removed from their crowded dwellings."

It will be seen, I think, even from this imperfect indication, that to any woman as capable, conscientious, and large-minded as Mrs. Sheldon Amos, Vestry work offers an extremely interesting field of labour, and I cannot but think that from the disinterested services of such women our London Vestries will eventually be the gainers.

MRS. BURGWIN.

(From a photograph by the London Steroscopic Co., Regent-street, W.)

THE EDUCATION OF DEFICIENT CHILDREN.

MRS. BURGWIN.

THERE IS A SPECIAL TYPE of human Calamity with which we are all acquainted in the family life of the wealthier classes. The Calamity to which I refer is usually described as " a child not quite like other children." The words are whispered about the drawing-room in the women's half-hour after dinner. Then the existence of the Calamity is partly forgotten. But meantime the years of infancy—years that the miserable parents would only too gladly prolong—pass away. With the minimum of publicity the Calamity is one day removed to an " establishment for delicate and backward children," as its proprietor euphemistically terms it. During the period that now elapses the Calamity is so ingeniously dealt with, that—Nature co-operating in the most meagre degree— it can ultimately be presented to the world as no Calamity at all. It never, certainly, makes any pretension to cleverness (a quality, at the best of times, easily mistaken for something different), but it can say and do what other people do and say, and thus passes through life as an inconspicuous, if not precisely a useful, member of society; which is assuredly a much happier lot than that of the outcast, which Nature had apparently intended it to be.

But whilst we have exhausted endeavour in dealing with these Calamities of the wealthier classes (the descent of titles, historic names and estates being often involved in the result), we have ignored the Calamities of the poor. We have treated these deficient or—as Sir Douglas Galton terms them—"abnormal" children as though they were precisely like other children. We have driven them into the board schools and placed them in the crowded classes and taught them as though they had the full use of the ordinary mental and physical faculties. Unmistakable imbeciles have no doubt been relegated to the asylums, but only a small proportion have had (can I say?) the good fortune to be admitted there. It is but the other day that, visiting a school in one of the poorest quarters in the East End, my eye fell on a considerable number of children who were manifestly unfit to be where they were. Some of them looked terribly ill merely, but most of them were sunk in a kind of stupor—the effect that the routine of an organised crowd produces on its most helpless members.

A SCHOOL FOR SPECIAL INSTRUCTION.

But to these unhappy children help is coming. " Schools for Special Instruction " are being rapidly established by the London School Board. There are fifteen of these schools already (including the Hugh Myddelton, recently opened by the Prince of Wales), and seven others will be ready immediately, so it is hoped that there will soon be no considerable district of the metropolis without such a training place.

It was at one of these schools—the Sayer-street Centre, on the south side of the river—that I met Mrs. Burgwin, and was permitted to inspect the classes under guidance. Let it suffice if for the moment I only mention that Mrs. Burgwin is superintendent of all the special schools—a statement which carries with it the inference that she is a lady of remarkable capacity. It was not until the close of our interview that I persuaded Mrs. Burgwin to tell me anything about herself, but I recognised from the first moment of greeting that I was in the presence of an extremely able and also of an extremely sympathetic woman.

Mrs. Burgwin led me immediately into the class-rooms. Visiting the lowest class first, we found some six or seven children (all boys, I think, though boys and girls were taught together) engaged in stringing beads, with bits of coloured paper placed at short intervals. The children were the most deplorable-looking of human creatures. They were to the ordinary observer scarcely distinguishable from idiots, and their bodies were evidently penetrated with horrible disease. In this lowest class were visible— only, of course, in an extreme degree—certain imperfections that showed themselves in almost every pupil. Squinting was the rule, the utterance was generally affected, the head and jaw were almost invariably misshapen. One poor little fellow had a jaw like a bulldog's, and from this cause, presumably, was almost speechless; he gazed at one with an animal's look of dumb suffering.

"Now, Tom," said Mrs. Burgwin to one of the children, as she moved the beads slowly along the string, "let me hear you count." The child, not looking at the beads, began to gabble the numbers vacantly. Mrs. Burgwin corrected him, making him touch the chain bead by bead. Then she questioned another as to the colours of the beads, and obtained more or less satisfactory replies. "Just notice their hands," she said aside to me; "you will see that their fingers are all short and stubby at the ends, except that boy's yonder. His fingers are very long and pointed. That is the only really vicious boy in the class. His face, no doubt, does not look a bad face to you, but I am familiar with it now as a common criminal type. I am afraid we shall not be able to keep him"— a forecast that the object of these remarks strengthened just then by putting some of the beads into his mouth. Meanwhile, it was touching to see these deplorable little creatures holding up their handiwork to Mrs. Burgwin and to me, with the same innocent expectation of compliment that any pretty petted child exhibits. Then one of the biggest boys, with a queer kangaroo-like movement, due to a malformation of the legs common to this class, ran to open the door for us, and we passed into another room. Here a large party of children were learning to colour geometrical patterns with chalks.

"Now, this little girl," said Mrs. Burgwin, "is evidently improving. She is placing her strokes one beside the other in a common-sense way. It seems a very little thing, no doubt," she went on, "but in schools like this, we observe all kinds of little things that in other children are taken for granted. To see the simplest thing done rationally gives us immense pleasure."

In the next class-room the teacher was drawing a design of oranges with flowers and foliage in coloured chalks on the blackboard. The design was afterwards sketched on card for the children to fill in with colour, then perforate the outlines and stitch these with wool. One little girl was lying on her back, but stitching diligently all the same, and several children in this room were only sickly and ailing, though the majority were mentally deficient. I observed that two or three of the older pupils were making beautiful macramé work, and Mrs. Burgwin told me that she hoped to find employment for the cleverest of these children in a trimming warehouse. But naturally, she could not often expect to bring her charges up to a wage-earning standard; she could only endeavour to develop the clouded minds a little by appealing to them through the organs of sense and touch.

How Special Schools were Started.

By this time the children were tired of their sedentary occupations, and were allowed to run off to the play-ground for a game of ball. It was then that I obtained a few quiet minutes with Mrs. Burgwin, and I availed myself of them to ask how she had been drawn into this work.

"I was mistress of the Orange-street School in Southwark for seventeen years before my appointment to this post, and it was there that I came in contact with a large number of this miserable class of children. My earlier years as a teacher were spent at St. Luke's, Chelsea, and at West Ham. In both these schools I had to deal with superior girls of the working class, so that the state of things which I found in Southwark made all the greater impression on my mind. We owe the origin of these special schools indirectly, I believe, to the Charity Organisation Society, which stimulated the Government to appoint the Royal Commission. But I consider that we are chiefly indebted to General F. J. Moberly for the vigour with which the scheme has been carried out. The General, as a member of the commission, was greatly impressed with the need for special schools of instruction; and, as vice-chairman of the London School Board, he was able to persuade that body to take the reform in hand. He is now chairman of the special committee of the board that manages our schools, and I can hardly tell you how much we are indebted to him for the active interest he shows in the work."

"When were the first centres opened?"

"In the summer of 1892. During the early months of that year I was gathering knowledge by a tour through France, Germany, Denmark, and Norway, when I visited some of the principal schools for dull children. Prior to that I spent some time in seeing the educational work carried on in our home asylums. The institutions which I most admired abroad were those of Dr. Keller, at Copenhagen, a private undertaking—where, by the way, I found some of the boys plaiting baskets for the London market!—and the Thorshang Institute at Christiania, which has lately been taken over by the State. In all the schools I visited, the body and mind are developed by manual training and physical exercises. In Germany a great point is made of gymnastics."

TEACHERS AND TAUGHT.

Having, in my survey of the classes, been charmed with the bright pleasant manner of the teachers, I asked Mrs. Burgwin whether it was not difficult to persuade women of this high calibre to undertake such painful work.

"We are obliged," was the answer, "to offer £10 more salary than the teachers would get in the ordinary elementary school, and, of course, we choose the teachers with special regard to their fitness for such posts. The strain upon their nerves and health is very great. I felt it myself indeed so much at first that I doubted whether I could go on with it. But as soon as I began to see the children improve (and their progress has been most marked) I began to take courage. We have been stimulated, too, by excellent reports from the Inspectors."

"How did the parents regard this effort on behalf of their children?" I inquired. "Oh, they were very glad indeed of the schools," answered the superintendent. "The worst of it is they consider they have a right to send us their children, however imbecile, and are sometimes very indignant when I tell them we can really do nothing with some particular child. They know, of course, poor things, that it is almost impossible to get the children into Earlswood, which is constantly full. Some mothers bring us one rickety child after another; and although the ricketiness often runs through a family of brothers and sisters, one cannot always trace hereditary causes, except that the marriages of cousins often turn out badly. I cannot find any theory of heredity proved in the instances that come under my notice, but in the course of my work I am daily faced by some very grave problems."

F

PHYSICAL TRAINING.

MME. BERGMAN ÖSTERBERG.

PROFESSIONS, like all things human, have their period of
rise and their period of fall. First they wax and wax, and
then they wane and wane. It is my aim in this series of articles
to draw the attention of those who are good enough to give it
rather to the professions which have a future than to those that
have only a past, be that past never so brilliant. Friends of
women's employment, more well-meaning than far-seeing, have
too often encouraged girls to enter professions of a decadent
character or of an extremely limited scope. It is high time, in
my opinion, that upon the gateway of such professions the
inscription were affixed "This is a blind alley."

Now, one of the professions with a small past and a big future
is that which formed the subject of a talk I had the other day with
Mme. Bergman Österberg. The teaching of physical exercises
was not a profession created by Mme. Österberg—when, indeed,
would it be true to assert that anybody had alone created anything?
for we in this country had long been feeling our way, *viâ* dancing
and dumb-bells and German gymnastics, towards a scientific
system of bodily development. But Mme. Österberg, when she
came to England from the Royal Institute of Gymnastics at Stock-
holm, came as the right woman at the right moment, for she
brought with her a well-defined code of educational principles,
and a strong personal determination to make others accept it.
Faith in her high ideal, and an iron resolution to attain it, are
Mme. Österberg's dominant characteristics. She is, in the best
sense of the term, a strong-minded woman, and the influence
exerted upon her pupils at the Hampstead Physical Training
College is no negligeable quantity in the educational forces of our
time. Before establishing herself at the institution in Broadhurst

MME. BERGMAN ÖSTERBERG.

From a photograph by Thos. Fall, 9 and 10, Baker-street, W.)

Gardens, however, Mme. Bergman Österberg had, as I knew, worked for many years in connection with the London School Board. Our talk began by reverting to that period.

One Education for Poor and Rich.

"Is it not rather funny," asked Mme. Osterberg, smiling, "that here in England you think what is good for the poor cannot be good for the rich? You know that when I was appointed Superintendent of Physical Education to the School Board (in succession to Miss Löfving) in 1881, I worked for six years to introduce the Swedish system of physical training into London schools. It was a great opportunity, and I was only too glad to take it. And I had the satisfaction of feeling that I succeeded, for during these six years I trained a thousand teachers, and introduced the Ling system into three hundred girls' schools. By that time I found that I had completed my task; the teachers I had trained would train others, and my work had received many flattering marks of approval. But the system had become identified with the education of the poor; that was the difficulty! Because, if it was a good education for the poor, it could not possibly be the same for the rich."

"Though, if it had been found good by the rich, the poor would have made no objection," I remarked. "No, very likely not. However, this argument did not impede me long. I built this college and gymnasium in 1885, and since then I have been working steadily to improve the physical development of women in the upper and middle classes."

A Choice of Two Careers.

"And, as in the case of the Board Schools, you accomplish your purpose by the training of teachers?" "Yes, and I can find posts for my pupils as soon as ever they are trained. Several posts, indeed, are standing vacant now until I have teachers to fill them. It is an excellent career for girls—regarded even only from the material side, for I stipulate that none of them shall take less than £100 a year, and many who are gifted and clever receive more. One of my former pupils has lately gone to the St. George's Training College in Edinburgh, another is at a large school in York, a third is at Port Elizabeth; but to tell you where they are all engaged would be only to give you a long list of the principal colleges and schools for girls.   Some of them, too, are acting as masseuses."

"Do the masseuses receive a different training from that of the teachers of physical exercises?" I inquired.   "Oh, no.   All undergo the same course of training for two years.   Massage and medical gymnastics are taught to all, for one of my teachers' most important qualifications is the treatment of girls with a tendency to spinal curvature.   This tendency is often curable by a proper system of muscular movements."

THE DAY'S ROUTINE.

Mme. Österberg told me presently that she provided board and lodging for many of the pupils during the two years' course.   This led me to inquire tentatively whether the Principal had any views on the questions of dress and diet.

"Views? yes, indeed, I have views," said Madame, with un-mistakable decision.

"What about petticoats?" I murmured, a day of mud and slush bringing this question into uncomfortable prominence.

"Oh, no petticoats.   We wear black tights under the dress, which must be short."

"And stays?" I interrogated.   "No stays either."

"And what are your rules about diet?"—"Plenty of wholesome food," said Madame; "plenty of fruit and vegetables, meat three times a day, and a properly regulated scale of diet which includes all the necessary flesh and bone-forming ingredients.   I am opposed to the drinking of much tea, and especially of strong tea."

"Any wine or beer?"   "No; what should they want with either if they are strong healthy girls, as I insist that they shall be?   I do not undertake to train delicate, unhealthy-looking girls, and I make it a point that no pupil shall begin her course who is not in a proper state of health.   Her teeth, for instance, if decayed, must be filled, or she must have artificial ones.   The hair and skin, too, must be in a wholesome condition.   But perhaps you would like to know the day's routine?"

I gladly assented.   Whereupon Mme. Österberg told me that the girls rose early and came down in their gymnasium costume to breakfast, which consisted of porridge and milk, coffee, a choice of meat dishes, and jam or marmalade.   After breakfast, the pupil-teachers would proceed to the gymnasium to teach the children (for whom special classes are provided), and to be taught themselves—the course consisting always of a lesson of theory alternating with a practice lesson. Special stress in the curriculum is laid upon lecturing, for, as Mme. Österberg truly observed, "a teacher who can only do things herself, and cannot explain the why or the wherefore, is really no teacher at all."

"In the warm weather," continued Mme. Österberg, "the pupils refresh themselves after their morning s work by a swim in the swimming-bath opposite. At one o'clock we have dinner— a good substantial meal of three courses—soup, meat, and pudding. During certain hours in the afternoon the girls are free to go out where they please. I leave them absolute liberty in this matter. At six they have tea. In summer our arrangements are a little different. Then we have tea early, and the girls go out a little distance by train to a cricket field that I have, where they play cricket and other games till the eight o'clock supper. Fencing, too, forms one of our regular subjects. In the evening we have a couple of hours' study, and from nine to ten we have a social evening, dancing, or debate. At ten all are to bed."

THE ULTIMATE IDEAL.

Thus we continued to talk, but athwart all that was said I caught a ray of light shed from some brighter ideal beyond. I perceived that Mme. Bergman Österberg, like most remarkable people, is not working *nur in den Tag hinein*, not contenting herself with a succession of daily rounds, however well accomplished, but pressing always forward and onward. And the goal of her efforts is the development of the minds of women, the attainment of the healthful mind through the increased health of the body.

" The girls when they leave me are altogether different creatures, their physical capacity has developed surprisingly; but what is far more striking is the improvement in mind and character. They have come to a better understanding of the facts of life and nature, and of their own place in the world. They have got rid of sentimental morbid fancies, if they have ever had any, and they have become responsible human beings." That is why I have said already Mme. Bergman Österberg is an educational force.

STOCKBROKING.

MISS AMY E. BELL.

FOR seven years Miss Bell has been a stockbroker, and during the greater part of that time the only lady stockbroker in this country. Why is this? Why should one woman open the road that leads to financial business, and why have other women not hastened on this, as upon other occasions, to follow the successful pioneer?

How Miss Bell Became a Stockbroker.

I think the second part of my question will answer itself when I have offered to the first the reply which Miss Bell gave me as we sat the other day—she and I—in her office hard by the Stock Exchange. It was by an incident of her childish days that Miss Bell made me understand better than by a longer explanation what had drawn her into her special line. An old gentleman, a visitor to Miss Bell's home at Bristol, happened one day to be diligently reading the money article in the *Times*, and in no mood for interruption from the child beside him. "Run away, little girl," he said, "I am busy with my lessons, and you must go to yours." "Ah," replied the child ingenuously, "but what's *your* lessons is *my* play!" The small Miss Amy, it seems, used to think it her highest recreation to study the quotations of the Money Market, and to note the rise and fall in various kinds of stocks and shares. I am able to dispose of the idea, which has somehow gained currency, that Miss Bell stepped into a stockbroking business left her by a relation. That was not so. Her business is of her own making, and although from time to time she has received valuable information and counsel from one or two leading firms—a fact she most gratefully acknowledges; she would not, I suspect, have been thus befriended if she had not

Amy Elisabeth Bell

(From a photograph by Messrs. H. S. and H. E. Mendelssohn, 14, Pembridge-crescent, W.)

possessed the highly trained ability and absolute integrity of character that always command the respect of the City. I name these qualifications rather than others I might mention—such as an unusually distinguished career at University College, Bristol, and her attainment of a Goldsmiths' Scholarship, which took her to Newnham College—because intellectual achievements are wont to weigh light in commercial scales. But there is a disqualification as well. No woman has yet been admitted to the Stock Exchange ; consequently Miss Bell remains an outsider, but with this difference—while outsiders, as a rule, advertise largely, and scatter their circulars broadcast, she does not advertise at all, and takes no speculative accounts whatever.

QUALIFICATIONS FOR THE BUSINESS.

"You need to begin afresh every day," says Miss Bell, in speaking of the difficulties of her business. By this expression I take her to mean that the work cannot be performed in instalments, as a man writes a book, with a chapter yesterday and another to-day. "And then," she continues, "you must do every-, thing yourself. You must read a great deal—books of history and political economy chiefly—but the newspapers continually. Keep an eye on the colonies and these newly explored African territories, did you say? Yes, indeed, and not one eye, but a dozen if you had them! The chief qualifications for a successful stockbroker are, in my opinion, a keen interest in the world's affairs and sympathy with individuals. The attitude of the superior person who stands aloof from this, that, or the other subject of the moment, will do him or her no good in this profession. A man or woman with half the education of the superior person, and a bright, active mind, will do far better in the City. By sympathy with individuals, I mean the power of understanding your client's position. If, for instance, a woman writes to me and says she is old and a widow, that her family are comfortably settled in life, and that she wishes to make sufficient provision for the rest of her days, I know pretty well what kind of investment would suit her best. But if she gives me none of these personal details, I may not succeed in pleasing her half so well. Of course, in one sense a good security is always a good security, and whether the holder is old or young has nothing to do with the question, but from another point of view several things have to be considered in the placing of money besides the yield of any particular investment. On the whole, I find that women do not generally write so fully as men. Women's business letters are often brief to the point of curtness. If a client can put much information into little space so much the better; but if she cannot, it is far wiser to write at length than not to put the broker in possession of all essential facts. But an interview is more satisfactory, when it can be arranged, than correspondence, however adroitly conducted.

" With regard to the qualifications of a stockbroker, I should say that early training is a great help. In my own case such training was not to be obtained, and for some years I felt the want of it. I could not, as a young man could, enter a stockbroker's office as a clerk, and so become gradually initiated into the work of each department. A woman cannot obtain this kind of experience, and, besides experience, capital is required. I should advise no woman to think of this career unless she had sufficient means to live upon, quite independent of business profits."

How a Woman Stockbroker can Help Women.

As our conversation proceeded, I began to perceive that in Miss Bell's case, as in that of other women who have entered professions hitherto filled only by men, the ultimate goal might appear to be the same for both sexes, but was in reality quite different. In medicine, in teaching, in journalism, in all professions which are carried on not in the solitude of the studio or the study, but out in the crowded world, by means of direct human intercourse— in such professions as these women do not oust men from their places, but they make places for themselves that men have hardly known to be places at all. Now, Miss Bell, for instance, finds the majority of her clients among women. She is able to help her particular *clientèle* in ways that the ordinary stockbroker in a large business would hardly think of or contemplate. A woman with a hundred or two saved, may be, from her own professional earnings, scarcely dares to ask the big, successful stockbroker to invest the small amount for her, still less does she dare to occupy his time in consultation ; but the affair interests Miss Bell, not merely because her client is a professional woman like herself, but for another reason.

"I want," she says, "to make women understand their money matters and take a pleasure in dealing with them. After all, is money such a sordid consideration? May not it make all the difference to a hard-working woman when she reaches middle life whether she has or has not those few hundreds? As a whole, I find women are delightful clients, sensible, punctual, and courteous; but, of course, there are exceptions; some are at once both cautious and reckless. They are reckless in taking what I may term 'dinner-table advice.' They meet a gentleman at dinner— an entire stranger—who tells them that some mine or another is doing wonderfully well. Forthwith they put their money down that mine, and probably never see it again. On the other hand, sooner than buy something in the market in the ordinary way, they sometimes persist in applying direct for shares in a new company with an alluring prospectus, whereby they think to save the stockbroker's fee. Then they dilly-dally over trifles. They will let a good investment escape them, if the dividends are paid in January and July, when they wish to receive them in April and October. On the whole, I certainly find that the rich women understand their financial affairs better than the poor. But this ignorance is very general. Many women are quite astonished when I explain business details to them, and ask, 'But is that really all?' So many women, you see, are not allowed to have the command of their capital. But in this, as in other ways, I rejoice to see that women are daily becoming more independent."

As my immediate purpose is only to report what professional women say about their professions, I ought perhaps to end here, but it would give an inadequate idea of Miss Bell s public spirit should I fail to add that much of her leisure is devoted to the encouragement of several admirable forms of thrift for women, and that she places much valuable advice at the service of those who invoke her aid.

ACCOUNTANT AND AUDITOR.

MRS. HAROLD COX.

"EQUAL PAY FOR EQUAL WORK!" is a cry which men raise with painful persistence whenever the subject of the woman's wage comes uppermost. But these unhappy victims of the feminine competitor too frequently resemble the Tennysonian infant in having "no language but a cry." For, if they really wished to compel woman to offer her goods at the same price as their own they would surely invite—nay, urge—their under-selling rival to join whatever societies they have formed for raising the status of the trades and professions; or, in more prosaic terms, for raising wages. If they omit to do this, it can only be assumed that the grievance is an imaginary one, and that women are free to make whatever terms they individually find remunerative. There can be no doubt which of these courses is the wiser; but if there were, a consideration of the medical profession, in which women scrupulously abide by the customary scale of fees, would set it at rest.

It might appear odd therefore if, amongst a body of such businesslike men as the accountants, any hesitation should be felt, especially as their Institute only obtained its charter of incorporation within recent years. At the time, however, when the charter was framed, the approaching entry of women into the profession was not foreseen, and the document, it appears, was worded in such a manner that nothing short of a supplemental charter could enlarge its scope, so as to make it applicable to both sexes.

Meanwhile women labouring under the disadvantage of their inability to style themselves "chartered" accountants are confronted with the expectation of clients that they should accept lower terms than men. It is difficult for them to decline; at the

MRS. HAROLD COX.

(From a photograph by Flemons, Tonbridge.)

same time, in yielding they must eventually reduce the general rate of remuneration. Professional loyalty, however, flourishes among the best women, even under the most adverse conditions, and I would gladly believe that the majority of women accountants follow the example of Mrs. Harold Cox and steadfastly decline all work that is not offered them upon the same terms as it would be offered to a man. This is with Mrs. Cox a simple matter of principle. But were it otherwise, I believe she would still consider herself bound to pursue the same course in recognition of the kindness she received from individual accountants when, as quite a young girl—before her marriage with Mr. Harold Cox, the well-known writer—she began to learn the mysteries of the business.

One day, when I found myself in her picturesque home in Gray's-inn, I was encouraged by the deceptive air of old-world repose to ask Mrs. Cox to tell me the story of her career from the beginning. She demurred on the score that it really was not much of a story, that other women accountants could tell me a better, and was, in short, as able people are, much too modest. But I urged the plea that young women thinking of this calling would be helped by knowing how she had entered upon it, and Mrs. Cox, always most generous where the welfare of other women is concerned, kindly waived her personal hesitations.

Lessons From Many Masters.

By way of introduction, I then asked what had turned her mind in this particular direction. "It happened," she said, "that when I was about fifteen, some friends of ours failed in business, and it was admitted that their failure was in great measure caused by their inattention to accounts. I was at that time wishing very much to earn something more than a young girl's pocket-money, and eventually to make myself independent, so I made up my mind to learn book-keeping."

"And how did you set about it?" "Oh, at first it was not difficult. I discovered that there was a book-keeping class at the College for Working Women in Fitzroy-street. It is to the college I owe my initiation. The teacher was not only a competent but an extremely kind man, and, seeing how anxious I was to learn, he gave me valuable help privately as well as in class. From

Fitzroy-street I proceeded to the College for Men and Women in Queen's-square. Here I had the fortune to find a teacher who was equally good to me. After going through the Queen's-square curriculum and receiving much individual help, I felt that I had learnt about as much as can be taught in book-keeping classes. I visited, however, the Birkbeck Institute for a time, and enlarged my knowledge by observing what questions were asked by students, and how they were answered. In the meantime I had taken the Society of Arts examination, and had passed second class; and a little latter I took it again, and this time came out among the firsts."

"Being one of the handicapped sex, you could not, I suppose, become an articled pupil to an accountant in the usual way?"
"It would have wanted a courageous accountant to take me," Mrs. Cox replied; "but, short of this, members of the profession have done much more to help me than one might have expected. I shall always particularly remember the kindness of an accountant in permitting me to see how he did his business. This gentleman allowed me on one occasion to accompany him when he went to a shop to examine the books. He introduced me as his clerk, but I recollect that the youths sitting on their high stools in the counting-house were overcome with laughter on seeing a woman amongst them. I learnt something that day; in particular not to be over-anxious (as I generally am) when accounts will not come right the first time. There was an item in the book which could not be explained. This would have made me miserable, and I was amazed when my friend said, in the easiest tone, ' Well, we will leave it for a month, and then perhaps it will come right;' and sure enough it did."

"And what happens when mistakes decline to come right of themselves?" "Oh, then it is awkward, even for the calmest accountant. It happened once that a firm of solicitors—quite a celebrated firm—were unable to account for a sum of three guineas in a balance-sheet that they were auditing. Though the sum was small, they felt that their credit demanded they should account for it. Seeing me by chance at the time, they asked me —though with very little hope—whether I could find the missing sum. And by great good luck I did. The firm acknowledged my little service in the handsomest way; but they requested—and this amused me—that I would sign my name to the statement as

H. Clegg (my name before my marriage), not Helen Clegg. You were asking, though, how I learnt the business, and I have not finished telling you. For, in reality, I am still learning. At the very beginning, I made a practice of asking any business men I met to explain matters to me that I did not understand, and the explanations, which were readily given, I wrote down immediately in note-books. This plan has been of great service to me."

Women's Financial Failings.

"Of the accountant, then, it may be said that all money matters are her province?" "Certainly," replied my friend, "no knowledge on the subject comes amiss. But how desperately ignorant many of us women are about such things! I find this ignorance shown in a variety of ways. There are women, for instance, who will enter into a partnership, and on learning at a given moment that their share in the profits of the undertaking is worth such-and-such a sum, will imagine that the money, cash down, can be paid into their hands at once. They can scarcely be brought to understand that for the moment the sum is on paper only, and that it cannot be realised until good debts are paid some months hence."

"This augurs a shocking degree of matter-of-factness amongst us. But you meet also, I expect, with plenty of women whose minds are extremely vague on the subject of money?" "Yes," said Mrs. Cox earnestly, "and there are many women who on this account do not get the remuneration that they ought. A great many clever women unfortunately take no interest in their pecuniary affairs, and even when they are managing large undertakings are quite content so long as they have still a balance at the bank. I made the effort some years ago to awaken women (and men, if they need it!) to a livelier interest in their money matters. Have you ever seen my 'Investment Record Book?' This is it." And Mrs. Cox produced a little book, of which I believe many who have incomes derived from investments have dimly felt the want. The book, when filled up, forms a neatly tabulated record of the circumstances under which stock has been bought and sold, so as to show at a glance the loss or gain on the transaction; and I was not surprised to learn that it had had many purchasers.

NATURE OF THE BUSINESS.

Returning from this digression, I ask Mrs. Cox to tell me how she obtained her first engagement. "It was indirectly, as such things happen. I used to take part in some amateur theatricals for an East-end charity in which Miss Goold, of the College for Men and Women, was interested. Miss Goold, knowing that I had studied book-keeping at the college, asked me to overlook the accounts of the charity. I think that was how I began. At the present time I am accountant to various societies and private persons, but my principal employment is in connection with certain educational establishments. Mrs. Walter Ward (who, as you know, is a helpful friend to her own sex) has placed the accounts of her school in my hands for many years past. One day a week is devoted to visiting a large girls' school at Windsor, and I also keep the books for a school at Hampstead. These are the engagements which absorb most of my time."

And here, if any reader fondly imagines (as perhaps I did myself) that the accountant's duties are finished when she has added up two sets of figures and subtracted one total from the other, let me disabuse that innocent person's mind. The accountant does not find the figures before her, she has to discover them. She has to learn at a school, for instance, not only such main facts as the salaries paid to teachers, she must also learn what every girl ought to be paying in fees and in "extras." Imagine what it would mean to have to acquaint yourself, say, with the precise number of pupils who take milk for lunch, and you will have some idea of the mastery of detail required by a competent accountant.

IS IT A PROFESSION TO RECOMMEND?

Looking at the business simply from this point of view, I perceived it would not do for everybody, or rather, everybody would not do for it. I found that Mrs. Cox was chary of recommending it to the average girl who expects to earn two or three hundred a year after six months' training.

"To that class of young woman," she continued, "I give no encouragement. But in any case, an accountant occupies such a confidential position, and is made acquainted with such intimate private affairs by her clients, that I feel she ought to be a woman of much tact and judgment. This holds good no doubt of a man also. But you must remember that a man undergoes a long period of probation and discipline. He is usually articled for five years at a fee of about £300, and he only receives a small salary towards the end of that time. But ultimately the fact of his having received the recognised training and become probably a " chartered " accountant is the best guarantee of his qualifications in the public eye. A woman must trust at the outset entirely to her personal qualities, though conscientious work is, in the end, her best recommendation. That is why I lay so much stress upon character."

PRINTING.

MISS WEEDE.

THE ASSOCIATION OF IDEAS between a commercial enterprise managed by women and a handsome dividend is not at all so remote as some scoffers would have us believe. Such an association is offered to the view in the Women's Printing Society, a business which continues to yield its shareholders interest at 5 per cent., and to give both shareholders and *employées* substantial bonuses. The fire a couple of years ago (1893), which destroyed the society's premises at Westminster, necessitated the removal of the business to a new domicile; but this expensive circumstance notwithstanding, the business continues to prosper, and the board of lady directors (amongst whom are Louisa Lady Goldsmid, the Hon. Mrs. Vernon, and Miss Agnes Zimmermann) continues to grow in prosperity.

THE MANAGER.

A business does not develop from nothing into a considerable something without the services of an able manager, and such the society undoubtedly has in Miss Weede. When I found her in her office at 66, Whitcomb-street, near Piccadilly Circus, I asked Miss Weede to tell me, in the first instance, how her own connection with the affair came about.

"I am a printer's daughter," she said, "and this made me feel interested in printing; but I knew nothing of the trade practically till I came here some fourteen years ago to learn it. Mrs. Paterson, you know, started this society, and was its first manager. I worked under her for many years, learning all the details of the business, until upon her death I was appointed manager. That was about eight years ago."

(From a photograph by E. Pannell, Brighton.)

System of Employment.

"You take girls as apprentices?" I inquired. "Yes," said Miss Weede; "girls are apprenticed to us for three years, at a premium of £5."

"And do they earn anything during their apprenticeship?" "After the first three months we pay them 3s. a week, and every three months 6d. weekly is added, so that towards the end of the time they are receiving about 9s."

"And when the girls become skilled printers, Miss Weede, what are their earnings approximately?" "The 'stab wages are 28s. per week; but the earnings of the piece workers naturally vary according to the quickness of the individual. On an average, I should say that the piece workers make 25s. per week. Our 'stab rate is a little below that fixed by the trade union, consequently our workers are all non-unionists. But they have never expressed any wish to join the union. The union, however, I am happy to say, does not put our office on its "black list;" and, indeed, taking other things into consideration, I think the pay comes to very much the same as the union rate."

I asked what those other things were, and Miss Weede explained that the hours were short—9 a.m. to 6.30 p.m. "Then," she added, "there are the bonuses." These are apportioned (she went on to explain) according to the amount of each *employée's* weekly earnings. "Some of our cleverest women I have known to receive as much as £9 for the year's bonus. The directors, too, have made presents of shares to some of our hands, so as to increase their sense of direct participation in the fortunes of the business."

I hazarded the conjecture that, despite all these advantages, the girls doubtless were constantly surrendering the agreeable known for the hazardous unknown in the form of marriage.

"Oh, but indeed they are not," Miss Weede replied, with emphasis. "I believe only two of our printers have married during the eighteen years that the business has been established. It is certainly a proof that the work is congenial that our hands stay on with us. But the consequence is that we seldom have a vacancy, and are obliged to refuse many applicants for apprenticeship. Lately, however, we have increased our numbers, and at the present time we are employing forty women.

G

As, under the manager's escort, I wandered upstairs into the two composing departments (one for jobbing and the other for bookwork), and saw the young women setting up type, some with fingers plying extraordinarily fast, others picking out the letters more slowly, but all looking as though they enjoyed their occupation, I came to the conclusion that printing—or at least composing —was a capital employment for either sex. The literature which the women were setting up was, for the most part, connected with the women's interests of the day; and doubtless the growth of these interests in importance has led to the increased prosperity of the Printing Society. The weekly paper, the *Woman's Herald*, was printed by the society before it passed (as the *Woman's Signal*) into the hands of its present proprietors, and the firm now print for the Women's Suffrage Societies in Parliament Street and Great College-street; for both the Women's Liberal and Liberal Unionist Associations; also for Bedford College, Queen's College, Baker-street High School, and the Princess Helena College. The Theosophical Society's publications are also entrusted to the Whitcomb-street firm. In the reader's sanctum I found a woman who appeared to have satisfactorily solved the problem of looking to the sense without forgetting the type, and there is a lady book-keeper likewise.

A few men, however, are kept on the premises, so as not to leave that capable sex altogether out of account. It is these who work the machines—a task which is too heavy for women. Aroused to a feeling of chivalry at sight of this little band of machinists, I expressed to Miss Weede my hope that women would still leave some scraps of printing for men to occupy themselves with.

"There is not much fear of women ousting men at present," was the reply. "So long as women are forbidden to work at night, employers are likely to prefer employing men. Women can do some of the lighter and more mechanical work in a printing office; but at present there are scarcely any women who can be termed 'all-round' printers in London except those who have been trained here." I came away reassured. Women may still earn 30s. a week or so by type-setting without depriving Man of his right to support his family.

MISS ALICE HUGHES.

PHOTOGRAPHY.

MISS ALICE HUGHES.

A HANDSOME house in Gower-street. A footman shows me nto a double drawing-room, Persian carpeted, furnished with restful many-cushioned sofas; decorated, as to walls, with some fine pictures. This is hardly like a photographer's. Have come to the right address? Yes; Miss Hughes will be with me directly, I am told; she is engaged at this moment. So I perceive, for voices reach me from the further room. They are voices of the kind that foreign observers say are peculiar to English women of the upper ranks—soprano voices, clear, and at the same time very sweet. These ladies spend a long time in making an appointment with Miss Hughes—they are so busy. But at last there is a rustle of departing skirts, and Miss Hughes hurries into the room.

"So sorry to have kept you!" she exclaimed. "And I do not really know that there is much that I can tell you about this business; but there is just one thing that I wish you would impress upon girls who think of becoming photographers. And this is that they must begin at the beginning. Do try to persuade them that it is mere waste of money to open, say, a studio in Bond-street until they have mastered the business by going through all the regular stages. I make it a rule here only to employ girls who have already received some training, and who exhibit real aptitude.

"But where are the poor beginners to make their beginning?" I inquired, in some perplexity. "They cannot do better than attend the classes at the Polytechnic in Regent-street. I learned there myself in the first instance, and the teacher is a most able man. I am reluctant, however," continued Miss Hughes, with an air of graceful deprecation, distinctly uncommercial, "to refer to

my own career as offering any encouragement to others, for I
have undoubtedly enjoyed special advantages. My father is, as
you know, an artist, and it was in order to photograph his portraits (often desired for presentation to the subjects' friends) that
I studied photography. Yes, that is one of them," she said,
interrupting herself, as my eyes lighted on a full-length portrait
distinguished by an extreme softness and delicacy of tone.

"People liked these photographed portraits," Miss Hughes
continued, "and began to urge me to take photographs direct
from life. But for some time I hesitated, and even when I
yielded to these requests I began in quite a small way. I took
my photographs out in the garden, for I had no studio then, and
I did every bit of the work myself."

"But you do not now?" "No; I employ a large number of
people now, principally for developing, retouching, and spotting.
You shall see for yourself if you will come with me." So saying,
Miss Hughes leads the way to her studio, to reach which we have
to traverse a series of small compartments, where men are
superintending the various processes. We take a look in at the
packing room, where every inch of wall space is occupied with
stacks of photographs, pigeon-holed and alphabetically docketed.
Young women, I observe, are in charge of this room, and Miss
Hughes tells me that the head of the packing department occupies
a post of some responsibility, and must, accordingly, be well paid.
Next we glance in at the tastefully furnished dressing-room, and
finally we ascend to the top of the house, to discover about a
dozen girls busy "spotting."

Each girl has before her a set of incomplete prints, and a
model of the photograph as it should be. One print, for,
instance, exhibits an awkward high light just where it is least
desirable, in the centre of an elaborately curled fringe. The
spotter applies a little water colour with a camel's hair brush, and
the damage to the coiffure is instantly redressed. Spotting is
work that demands no high degree of skill, and girls, Miss
Hughes tells me, earn from 10s. to £1 a week. Their hours are
nine till six. Miss Hughes having previously told me that a
retoucher in a first rate house not infrequently makes his £300
and more a year, I inquired whether the spotters were not
constantly aspiring to become retouchers. The answer was

disappointing. Miss Hughes had found very little ambition amongst girls. But it is conceivable that the girls' ambition may be rather thwarted than non-existent owing to the remissness of parents in teaching their daughters a trade.

Miss Hughes, however, is of opinion that girls could rise to higher things in photography if they tried. " But the longer I live, she observed, "the less I expect from anybody. Everyone has some flaw; one is lazy, another is inartistic, a third has no business capacity. One must just make the best of one's materials. I receive odd requests from would-be pupils sometimes. It is not often that I take a holiday, for my work sometimes occupies me from half-past seven in the morning till midnight. However, this summer I was at the sea for a short time. One morning, whilst I was bathing, a lady—a complete stranger—swam up to me and exclaimed that she wished to learn photography, and between the trough of one wave and the crest of the next she endeavoured to settle the matter ! "

I suggested that photography must be prolific in revelations of human foibles. " Yes, indeed," Miss Hughes assented. " Everybody must be young and beautiful. Women of fifty expect me to make them look no more than five-and-twenty, and stout women insist on being taken full length and represented as perfectly sylph-like. There are circumstances when the photographer is compelled to hint that she cannot do justice to her clients in the conditions they exact. But it is a very delicate matter to make such explanations." The occasions for painful truth-speaking must nevertheless be rare, for there is scarcely a beauty in English society who has not intrusted her fairness to Miss Hughes's camera, and as I turned the leaves of the album I saw face after face of acknowledged loveliness. And the children, too—what an immense improvement on the stiff little figures of twenty years ago are these pictures of spontaneous childish grace ! A little girl is playing peep-bo unconscious of observation, another holds up an apronful of flowers, and another fondles Negro, Miss Hughes's handsome black poodle. My eye was caught by an exquisite portrait of the Duchess of Portland with her children, and I recognised amongst photographs which have appeared in the illustrated papers, those of the Countess of Dalkeith, Lady Henry Cavendish-Bentinck, and Lady Arthur Grosvenor, together with less familiar likenesses of the Duchess of Devonshire, Countess of Powis, Lady Cairns, Lady Grey-Egerton, and Lady Griffin. It is impossible to look at Miss Hughes's work without recognising that she is an artist as well as a photographer; the grace of pose and originality of treatment are peculiar to herself. But Miss Hughes's modesty will not permit her to take much credit for her achievements, and her final words were, "I can only say that all that I do is genuine photography. I never attempt work that pretends to be something different from what it is, for that is what I account to be bad art."

MME. KATTI LANNER.

(Photographed by the London Stereoscopic Company.)

BALLET DANCING.

MME. KATTI LANNER.

THE PANTOMIME BALLET was in full rehearsal. A long chain of girls was twisting itself into a spiral coil and again untwisting with a rapid watchspring movement, as, betwixt the beats of the music, I slipped past the dancers and arrived at the top of the large hall, where Mme. Katti Lanner was seated directing her company. Mme. Lanner smiled and greeted me, bade me sit down beside her, and then proceeded with the interrupted business. Meanwhile I had time to look about me, and, as I had never seen a ballet in its practising costume before, I found plenty to observe. And what do the *corps de ballet* look like in the daytime; are they at all so pretty as they look at night, or are they—well, plain? Those are the questions I feel mentally that you are asking me; but, do you know, the loveliness or unloveliness of facial feature is the last affair I noticed; in dancing it is so obviously a matter of inferior consequence. What struck me (it would have struck you also had you been there) was the vivacious, intelligent expression of nearly every face, and the disciplined grace of every figure. I use the term disciplined grace because the quality is quite other than natural elegance, existing in the happiest instances side by side with it, but more often alone. Each girl poses her body at every moment as though she were there and then to be photographed. She knows that her image is to be mirrored on the retina of thousands of spectators, not as a single image, but as one of a great number of figures executing in unison a series of sharply defined movements. It is the precision, the *netteté* of outline, that has to be studied and achieved.

The practising gear is absolutely businesslike. Only here and there do I detect a suspicion of finery in a silk or satin blouse.

Usually the bodice is of some ordinary woollen material, and a white cambric petticoat, trimmed with two or three frills and reaching to just below the knees, completes the costume, save for a pair of pink satin heelless sandals. The children (what ballet of Mme. Lanner's would be complete without a troop of little ones?) are frocked with even greater simplicity—a loose banded bodice and short skirt of pink print. Everybody, big and little, carries a stick. This stick in its time plays many parts. It may be a wand, a doll, a flower—what you will. It is the understudy for all the "properties."

But whilst I have been gazing at the dancers, lost in that kind of mesmeric brown study that a ballet somehow induces, various changes have been taking place. The ladies of the corps have retired to rest and (incidentally) to talk, whilst the children dance through a very pretty piece of dumb show. Mme. Lanner explains it to me:

"You see the little girl seated in the centre. That is Cinderella—this is our Lyceum ballet—you know, for the 'Cinderella' pantomime. Now you see the children are helping her to dress for the ball; they are handing her powder puffs, and mirrors—and see, now, they are fanning her." The children who are supposed to line the two sides of the stage, bend forward, fanning the air rhythmically (on this occasion they are provided with palm leaf fans), while Cinderella smiles a coy approval. Then there is a general gallopade, and the fans get rather in the way. "Never mind your fans, children," cries Madame in her pleasant, foreign tones, "they shall be all right by-and-by, when you will have them hanging at the side by ribbons."

Then the children sink into picturesque attitude to form a final tableau. But Madame's quick eye fastens upon a child who does not contribute her share to the general effect. "Ah! you little Miss ——!" she exclaims. "You are a naughty girl. Kneel upon your right knee, not the left; and what is your arm doing there?" Madame beckons to her assistant teacher. "Please put Miss —— into her proper position. So, that is better. But you must take care next time, or you will have to go." In an aside to me, Madame whispers, "We shall have tears, I am afraid; the children cannot bear to leave the ballet"; but the little breeze blows over, for the small people, I suspect, know that Mme. Lanner, though an absolute monarch, is a most kind-hearted one.

"There, that will do, children," says Madame, giving an extra pleasant smile to the whilom victim of disgrace, "and now, ladies, I am waiting for you." Whereat the ladies indicated advance, some holding waste paper baskets above their heads, others pretending to do so. "Ah! but you shall have such lovely baskets," says Madame. "You will be delighted with them. Take a flower from the basket—yes, like that," she adds in approval, as the girls, quick to seize the hint, wave a hand from the basket to their partners, who must be imagined as gallant swains. Then the girls glide back, leaving the centre free for all the children to come skipping forward, and a little later the ballet developes into a rapid whirling maze.

And so the rehearsal goes on; and there is no more end to the variety of the dance than to the variety of nature. But there is an end to the capacity of the dancers, who began at twelve, and it is now mid-afternoon. So Mme. Lanner dismisses the party, tells the *première danseuse* (who has just returned from an engagement in Paris) that she will be ready for her by the next rehearsal; and now I know that my time has arrived for a little quiet chat with the celebrated teacher.

A RAPID RETROSPECT.

Mme. Lanner amiably consented to exert, on my behalf, as much voice as the rehearsal had left her, and led the way to her private sitting-room over the big hall in Tottenham Court-road, where her National Training School practises. My first question was retrospective; I murmured the word "career" with a hint of apology, knowing I was asking for much.

"My career?" Madame shook her head. "Ah, but that would take too long! I have seen so much, done so much. I have danced in every capital in Europe; yes, and have been to America besides. My life has been full, immensely full; there has been plenty of interest and amusement and much hard work in it."

"You were a dancer, Madame, before you became a teacher?"

"Yes, indeed; I have danced with Fanny Elssler and Cerito. Those were the days of the good style of dancing. I began to learn in Vienna, where my father, the musical composer, lived.

I was only six when I received my first lesson. Then, as you know, I danced for many years, and conducted my ballet at the same time. But now the ballet is quite enough; for it is no longer one ballet, but several. I have organised ballets for Col. Mapleson at Drury Lane, for Mr. Carl Rosa, and for Sir Augustus Harris. At present my time is chiefly occupied with ballets for the Empire and the Crystal Palace; but I undertake a good many other commissions besides, as, for instance, this Lyceum dance that you have just seen."

Creating a Ballet.

"Do tell me, Mme. Lanner, how you design your ballets. There are no two of them alike, and yet those I have seen have been all lovely?"

"Now," said Madame, "how shall I explain? I really hardly know, for, properly speaking, I don't design my ballets at all. It happens in this way. The manager of the theatre—let us say Mr. Barrett—writes to me and says, 'I want a ballet for "Cinderella," and I should like to have introduced into it the idea of dressing Cinderella for the ball.' Or he says, if it is for the Crystal Palace, 'Our pantomime this winter is to be "Jack and the Beanstalk." Cannot we have children dressed as scarlet runners, and other children with rakes and watering cans.' The manager gives me just a hint or two of that kind—no more. I must fill in the rest. Well, then I think the matter over a little, and I say to the composer, 'Please give me so many bars to this movement, and so many to that,' my knowledge of music helping me very much here. But I settle no details until the ballet is before me. Then, somehow, one by one ideas come to me, and we add a little business here and a little there, till the whole dance is perfect."

"But all these preparations must surely take a long time?" I interjected.

"Oh, not so very long! Let me see, we have taken about six weeks for these two pantomimes. An Empire ballet takes longer; perhaps eight weeks. I have received a letter from the Empire only to-day asking me to begin a new ballet, although 'The Girl I Left Behind Me' has been running a very little while. But there must always be something fresh in readiness."

"And the dresses, Madame Lanner; have you anything to do with them?"

"No; Mr. Wilhelm designs them entirely, and very beautiful they are. What do I think about the present style of dancing dress? That depends upon circumstances. The short, full skirts that I was formerly accustomed to undoubtedly showed the finished dancer to the most advantage; still, I cannot deny that the clinging draperies and soft textures are becoming. The electric light, too, helps us somewhat at the present day, but for all our best coloured effects we use limelight."

IS BALLET DANCING HEREDITARY?

No; Mme. Lanner did not think it was, and Mr. Barker, the secretary of the school, demolished this popular fallacy with square facts.

"I should say," he observed, "that our dancers were chiefly the children of tradesmen, artizans, and *employés* of various kinds. They are not often the children of dancers.

"That is true," continued Madame, "but dancing may be said 'to run in families:' if one girl turns to dancing as a livelihood, her sisters will probably be only too glad to follow suit and thus help their parents. For instance, three little girls came here lately whose father had died by a sad misadventure. Knowing the hardship of the case, I placed all three at the Empire Theatre, in order that they should be able to earn as much as possible to support their mother and themselves."

Of the salaries I presently received details calculated to make many wish they could foot it featly. From the living wage of 18s. the dancer rises to £3, and she may hope, if her talent brings her into the front row, to make £5 or £6 weekly. With regard to solo dancers, Mme. Lanner instanced one of her pupils, who is now engaged in the provinces at a salary of £15, which, with the addition of *matinées*, comes to £22 weekly. "You might say from £20 to £25," she added, "is a fair average salary for a good dancer." Then I asked at what age children began to learn, and how long they usually were in learning. To the first question I obtained the reply that ten now was the lowest age, and to the second that the children I had seen downstairs had only been in the school three or four months.

Our conversation, having taken this tack, was bound to arrive in a minute or two at the rock of the " half-timers." Madame's views (you have guessed them already) were that the children's earnings at pantomime time made a highly acceptable addition to the family Christmas stocking. " And as for the amount of time lost at school," put in Mr. Barker, " it is actually only four afternoons a week, for Saturday is a holiday, and the children are, anyhow, entitled to one half-holiday a week. I am busy collecting ' exemptions ' at this moment," and he showed me a letter in which a certain board school specified its willingness to dispense with some little girl's attendance. " Besides," he added, with a hint of special pleading, " why should a child who is in the fifth or sixth standard not be able to dance four afternoons in the week when, if she were older, but only in the fourth standard, she might be out earning her living?"

Once a Dancer always a Dancer.

Except on the score of health, I could urge no answer to this objection; and seeing how remarkably well and happy the entire corps de ballet looked, I held my peace. However, I endeavoured to assure myself that my eyes had not deceived me, by asking Mme. Lanner how she managed at such an influenza season as the present.

" Oh, my dancers are hardly ever ill," she rejoined. " I think it must be the exercise that prevents them from catching colds and epidemics. We only require to employ a few understudies. No; the only epidemic I have had to complain of lately is matrimony," she exclaimed, laughing. " Fourteen, was it not, Mr. Barker?"
" Yes, fourteen of the corps de ballet have married this autumn. But when they marry, they often wish to come back. Many is the letter I have had from a former pupil, telling me how dull she feels, her husband away at his business, and she left at home with nothing to do. I, too, when I take a holiday—and I have only had a fortnight this year—feel dull without my work. I teach here all day, and at night I superintend my pupils at the Empire. I get back to my home on Clapham Common (where there is such lovely air) at one in the morning. Then sometimes I become rather knocked up, and the doctor says, ' Now, Madame, you must really take a day's rest.' I obey. I rest in the morning and in the

afternoon, but when the evening comes I pace up and down my house, feeling so restless, and longing to be at my post, that at last the doctor says, ' Well, Madame Lanner, if you cannot rest, I can do nothing for you. You had better go back to the Empire at once.' "

DOMESTIC TRAINING.

MISS PYCROFT.

IN the French passive sense, I was "assisting" one day at a conference on women's employment, when a lady, upon whose ears the words cookery and laundry work had fallen displeasingly, rose to protest against the o'erfrequent mention of those arts in connection with her sex. "Young women should not," she said, "have cookery and laundry work forced so insistently upon their attention"—or, as she more colloquially expressed it, "down their throats"—but should be offered a larger and more stimulating intellectual menu, comprising such dishes as algebra, history, and philosophy. In short she looked to the time when the girls should make conic sections and the boys blackcurrant jam, as the Cambridge wit put it. But, anyhow, she was very urgent that the boys should make the blackcurrant jam and felt that for boys this domestic training would be the very thing.

Whereupon Miss Pycroft, the organising secretary of Domestic Training to the London County Council, rose, and quietly observed that, as a matter of fact, classes in cookery for boys were being held, and that, personally, she entertained no prejudice regarding the sex to whom such knowledge should be imparted. She only thought it desirable that, as we still needed dinners, clothes, and other such material things, some persons of whatever sex should learn how to make them. With Miss Pycroft's introduction of sound sense, I noticed that a great peace fell upon the assembly, and the question of domestic training was settled for the time being. I recall this incident because it is characteristic of the attitude of reasonable recognition towards the main facts of life, which in Miss Pycroft's case accompanies a marked capacity for energetic action.

General Outlook for Domestic Teachers.

It was with a similar recognition of actualities that Miss Pycroft met my inquiries concerning the prospects for women teachers employed under the County Councils. It is nearly two years since Miss Pycroft began, under the direction of the Technical Education Board, to organise the system of domestic training in London, and she is, therefore, now tolerably well able to judge what the position of affairs is likely to be in the immediate future. "The great rush for teachers," she said, "is at an end. In future it will be less easy for teachers to obtain posts than when the Customs and Excise Act of 1890 first put money at the disposal of County Councils for technical education ; indeed, I consider that teachers with second-class diplomas will stand but a poor chance at all."

"And the chances of promotion," I interposed, "do you consider them good?" "No; not as compared with other professions —High School teaching for example. Our domestic teacher has the advantage—at all events for the moment—of obtaining pretty easily a lectureship with a salary of £90 (which is what the London County Council offers, as well as an allowance of £5 to cover extra expenses), and she does not need to have had the High School teacher's expensive education. But it is easier to obtain such a post than to get promotion from it. At the best, she may be appointed superintendent of the women's department in one of the polytechnics, though other qualifications than a training in domestic economy are needed for these posts."

"And her salary then?" I queried. "Well, the lady superintendents in two of our London polytechnics are receiving what amounts to £200 a year ; that is to say a salary of £150 or £160 and the use of rooms, which brings the value of the income to the sum I have named. Now I scarcely expect that when the present technical education schemes have been carried out there will be more than ten polytechnics in London altogether. We have, by the way, recently organised a day school of domestic economy for girls.

Next in value to these superintendentships come the organising secretaryships under the County Councils. There are only now three or four paid women secretaries, though eventually

I hope there will be more, as the paid secretary is generally much more efficient than the unpaid ; and it is difficult for the paid male secretaries to do this part of their work without women helpers. About equal in value to these are the superintendentships under the London School Board. The commencing salary attached to these offices is £150. And then just below these appointments in value are the head teacherships of technical institutes for women, with salaries of about £120. But there is hardly anything in this department of teaching that at all approaches the remuneration of the head teachers of a High School."

"But the question of salaries is dependent upon the question of initial outlay, is it not ?   And I believe," I added, "the expense of a domestic teacher's training is small ? "

" Yes, the charge for a teacher's training in the Battersea Polytechnic was £21 for a fifteen months' course; and half the number of pupils are admitted free; the term of training has, however, lately been increased to two years, and the fee will, I expect, be raised proportionately."

How to Increase the Skilled Workers.

Then I asked Miss Pycroft whether she considered there would always be a sufficiency of pupils for County Council teachers, and whether the elementary educational system, which already embraces domestic subjects, might not eventually be so perfected as to leave little scope for instruction from another source.

" You see " explained Miss Pycroft, " we take the girls at the age when they leave the Elementary Schools, and I cannot say that we find them at all so thoroughly versed in domestic subjects as to require no further teaching.   With our dress-cutting pupils, for instance, it is a tolerably frequent experience to find that they cannot turn a hem without assistance.   No doubt the Elementary School classes are too large for the children to receive sufficient individual attention.   But in any case, the children's education is assumed to have been only elementary, and it devolves upon us, in common with the evening schools, to carry it on from this point.   Theoretically, perhaps, the evening school system might be extended to embrace all the girls in their teens who are living at home, but as a fact it does not.   Many girls who escape the

teaching of the evening schools, will go to a girls' club or
institute in the evening, and in that way we are able to get hold
of them. Then in isolated classes it is impossible to give a
training in cookery and laundrywork as thorough as in a school,
where the instruction is more continuous and the processes can be
carried on from day to day. In our Domestic Economy Schools
we overcome this difficulty, and the help given in food and clothing
enables the girls to continue long enough to learn the subjects
thoroughly; without this it is their inevitable tendency to drift
into poorly paid occupations so as to earn something at once. As
schools of domestic economy are likely to increase in number,
they will provide an opening for teachers, even if the peripatetic
classes decrease.

" Speaking of trades, is there not the objection that a girl might
learn her business quite as well as an ordinary apprentice? "
" No; I do not think so, because the apprentice is seldom taught
more than a part of the trade. At the same time I fully realise
the advantages of learning a business practically. It was on this
account that I lately called upon Mr. Debenham, of Debenham
and Freebody's (who are, as you know, very liberal-minded
employers), and Mr. Debenham has kindly taken some of our
girls for a year, after their five months at a Domestic Economy
School, and will put them through all the departments of the
dressmaking business. The girls will not receive any wages,
whereas if they were apprentices they would be earning something
at the end of six months. A fund for their maintenance, meanwhile, has been started through the kindness of the City
Companies. Several of our ex-pupils are now apprenticed by the
Merchant Taylors' Company at a school of dressmaking, and
will be competent to take places in first-rate houses."

COOKERY, LAUNDRY, AND DOMESTIC HYGIENE.

" Is there a good demand for cookery teachers? " I then
inquired. " Fairly good," was the reply. " The best cookery
teachers will no doubt find employment in the schools of cookery,
preferring the fixed salaries and constant employment to temporary
engagements. Some competent women might be advised to take
posts of a housekeeping character. One such lady has recently
been engaged at a London hospital, and if other hospitals

did likewise it would probably be to the advantage of the nurses' dietary."

"And laundry work?" "With this subject we do less well. At many of the places where we hold our classes, the constant supply of fresh water, upon which we naturally lay stress for good washing, cannot be obtained; so it is a difficult subject to manage. Hygiene, for the opposite reason, is the most popular. It requires no ' plant,' but only a competent lecturer. Our present teacher has her time quite filled up, and this spring we engaged others for temporary work."

A Board of Domestic Examiners.

"With regard to the teacher's qualifications, Miss Pycroft. Does the Technical Education Board favour one examination more than another?" "No; we merely ask for a diploma from some domestic training school recognised by the Education Department, in addition to previous experience as a teacher. But a Board has lately been established for examining the students in the various training schools of Domestic Economy in London which has the adhesion of all such schools but one; and though each candidate for employment must stand on her individual merits, I think in future it will be impossible to avoid feeling a preference for candidates whose diplomas have been obtained by passing an examination the standard of which we know. We are making it compulsory that all candidates shall pass an examination in ' education and method,' as well as in their special subjects."

So I left Miss Pycroft, feeling that girls should not rashly abandon their saucepans to boys at the very moment when bachelorships in the domestic arts are probably in store for them.

MRS. MONTROSE.

(From a photograph by Dinnia, 18, Park-row, Leeds.)

LAUNDRY WORK.

MRS. MONTROSE.

ACTON, if it wants a second name, might call itself the Washtub of London, and no other quarter, except maybe the adjacent Ealing, would dispute its right to the title. Almost every house in Acton—or at least in South Acton—is a laundry, and as you pass through the streets a concatenation of cleanly ideas is flashed from eye to mind by the aid of some such titles (I do not answer for precision of nomenclature) as the " Driven Snow," the " Hygeia," " All England's Laundry," the " Sanitas," and " Soapsuds." There are announcements of " Mangles kept here," " Ironing done," or, as a confession of somebody's failure, " This laundry to let on easy terms." However, it was not to survey laundries in general, but to visit one laundry in particular, that I threaded the streets of South Acton. The laundry of my search has an unsurpassably pretty name, the " Sweet Lavender." Its history is a brief one, for it only came into existence five years ago, when Mrs. Montrose—owing to one of those commercial disasters which befal so many at present—found herself and her husband face to face with poverty. In fiction, persons thus circumstanced invariably retire to a rose-embowered cottage in the country, where they wait upon themselves as much as the one faithful retainer will permit, and amuse themselves by talking over the past. The heroine of such a story in real life does differently. On the principle of "taking a hair of the dog," she goes into business on her own account—only her business is not the vague speculative City variety, but a particular business that concerns everybody's daily needs ; tangible, familiar, common even, if you will. So Mrs. Montrose, when the catastrophe came, bethought her of laundry work as a business which might yield profit to an educated and capable woman, and forthwith, despite the head-shaking of friends, to South Acton she repaired.   It was a plucky thing to do, for the career Mrs. Montrose has chosen means the renunciation of society, pleasant surroundings, and almost all the elements that decorate existence ; but Mrs. Montrose is plucky, and as she entered the room on the occasion of my call a glance at the bright, spirited face, and the alert, slender figure, so well set off by a lavender print gown and apron, told me that here was one whom misfortune could not vanquish.

From Small Beginnings.

" You knew something of laundry work, no doubt, before you started in business," said I.   " Where were you trained ? "

Mrs. Montrose smiled.   " This has been my training school.   I arrived here one day to find four hampers of clothes that friends had kindly intrusted to me, but I had nothing whatever to wash them in.   I was determined that, come what might, those clothes should be washed, if I had to send all over Acton to get the necessary materials.   And washed accordingly they were. Still, I do very much wish I had been taught the business; I should have been spared many mistakes and losses at the outset. Friends, as I was saying, gave me my first chance; but I draw my customers now chiefly from the general public.   The business has grown very satisfactorily; but you must remember I superintend every detail myself.   That is the secret of success.   Never leave your business, or your customers will certainly leave you !   That has been my experience.   It is almost impossible to take a holiday."

Opposed to the Factory Act, but in Favour of a Union.

" Would you tell me your views on that moot point, the extension of the Factory Acts to laundries ? "

" I do not at present see the possibility of reducing the hours to a limit of twelve daily.   At seasons of pressure we are obliged to work overtime—sometimes till nine, very rarely till ten.   I discourage overtime work as far as possible ; at the same time, I must say I think the young women are better employed here than they would be if they were idling about in the street and getting into mischief.   They do not go home when they leave here, and what is there for them to do in the evening in such a neighbour-hood as this?"

"What would be your attitude towards a laundresses' trade union?"

"I should be extremely glad to see one formed. But what I desire most is to have a union of employers, so that a scale of charges for laundry work could be fixed. At present the competition between laundries is terrible. But indirectly, I think, a laundresses' union would tend towards that result, for, as the union would fix a minimum scale of wages, it would no longer pay employers to engage inferior workers."

"You probably pay rather extra good wages."—"Yes, because I felt bound, on entering such a business as this, to try to turn out work as well done as it can be. Laundresses earn very good money, ironers in particular, some of whom I have paid 25s. and 30s. a week, and generally from 18s. to 24s. Even a little girl, a collar dresser, makes her 12s. a week. Women in the washing room make 2s. 8d. a day, which includes 2d. as beer money. Overtime is paid for at 3d. an hour."

What Ladies Can Do.

"And now, Mrs. Montrose, I am eager to know what openings you consider there are for ladies in this business; I have heard such diverse accounts."—"From my own experience," she replied—"and I have trained a great many ladies already—I must say there are capital openings. Of course my pupils have varied very much in ability, but I have seldom found any difficulty in getting them work at a salary of about a pound a week. One of my pupils, a lady, who was exceedingly clever, obtained a situation as superintendent in a large steam laundry at £80 a year, but she did not keep it long as she wished to return home. The head of the firm, however, offered to raise her salary to £150 if she would remain."

"It is as superintendents ladies are chiefly wanted, I believe?"
"Yes; but they may be asked to begin as assistant superintendents, or even as bookkeepers. The most responsible part of a superintendent's duties is to examine the women's lists of work, and see that they are correctly charged on the slate. Nearly all laundry work now is paid by the piece. One lady on leaving me

went out as an ironer; but this is a step not generally to be recommended, for ironing is heavy work."

I inquired what was the length of the course of training for ladies, to which Mrs. Montrose replied that three months was the usual time, and that she charged five guineas only for the teaching. One or two ladies, I may add, are permanently employed in the Sweet Lavender Laundry.

A Glance Round the Laundry.

The whirr of machinery in the background, which made an accompaniment to our talk, led me to ask if I might see the premises.

Mrs. Montrose willingly complied, taking me first into the washing room, furnished with the latest kind of steam boilers and rinsing machines, at which some women, two or three men, and a boy were busily employed. I observed that machinery did not appear to oust human beings altogether yet. "No; nor ever will," Mrs. Montrose answered; "at the same time, I as an employer, naturally prefer to use as much machinery as possible; and whenever anything new is invented, I make a point of seeing it at once. Shall I show you the ironing rooms? You will see they have been lately added to the house."

So saying, she led the way into two long rooms, where some four-and-twenty young women were ironing collars and the fronts of shirts, goffering lace frills, and folding clothes to go home. "I wish you had been here this morning," said the mistress of "Sweet Lavender," "for you would have seen a quantity of linen packed to send in our cart to Ealing. We take each district on a particular day." What I saw, however, was quite sufficient to convince me that Mrs. Montrose has amply deserved her success. As I looked at the piles of lovely snowy linen, I was reminded of a letter which I received the other day from one of Mrs. Montrose's customers. "Her work," said my correspondent, "is most beautifully got up; the colour of the clothes quite perfect, and flannel shirts and table linen all one can possibly wish. If," she added, in words which I cordially endorse, "there were more laundries managed by ladies, I think we should not hear so many complaints about the laundry as one meets on all sides nowadays."

MISS MARY E. RICHARDSON.

(From a photograph by Messrs. Elliott & Fry, Baker-street, W.)

STORE-KEEPING.

MISS MARY E. RICHARDSON.

A LADY may more easily learn any trade than Trade. That is only superficially a paradox. Every woman of the gentle class, who has endeavoured to penetrate the fastnesses of Trade, will understand me. She will understand that, whilst it is to-day comparatively easy for her to learn the trade—or shall I not rather say the handicraft—of dressmaking, millinery, confectionery, or whatever it may be, it has been up to this moment almost impossible for her to learn Trade itself—Trade, in the sense of purchasing, displaying, selling. and distributing commodities to the utmost advantage. The gentle class have only themselves to thank for their present difficulties. The gentle class have for so many centuries looked askance upon Trade, that Trade has at last replied in effect: "So be it; if you will have none of me, I will have none of you. But when the day comes that you wish to be on friendly terms with me, I, in my turn, will give you the cold shoulder. My secrets I will keep to myself; you may discover them some day, but you shall pay for your discovery dearly."

Such a day has come, and, as we know, the discovery of Trade's secrets has been to some a literally ruinous affair. Ladies, in particular, who have never known a single person in trade, or discussed a business matter in their lives, have plunged with foolhardy courage into trade of the very biggest kind, and, after a few years of seeming prosperity obtained by the reckless expenditure of their own and their friends' capital, their commercial existence has been expunged in the Bankruptcy Court.

Others there are who have bought their knowledge at great cost, but at something less than the price of failure. These ladies are now in a fair way to prosper, and it is only a matter of time for them to reap the harvest of their capital and labour. Amongst lady traders of this second class, Miss Richardson occupies a unique position. For Miss Richardson manages not merely a shop, but many shops in one. She is the principal shareholder and one of the directors of the Bedford Park Stores.

MISS RICHARDSON'S HISTORY.

Had I not found Miss Richardson in her managerial sanctum checking bills, had I not discovered her in an environment of eatables and drinkables, and the kindly fruits of a bountiful autumn ticketed with cash prices, I should have taken her to be a country lady ; I should have expected to hear of a well-managed estate, of a house and garden in splendid order, and of days spent pretty frequently in the hunting field. In making such a guess as this, I should scarcely have been far wrong, for Miss Richardson is a member of a well-known family in Lincolnshire—her brother is now M.P. for the Brigg division—and she passed her early days in the eastern county. But she found as she grew up that a country life was not to be hers (at least not a country life with sufficient scope for her energies), and she began to look about for some other source of interest.

"I thought seriously at one time," Miss Richardson said, " of going to Girton, but for one reason or another I did not succeed in carrying out the plan. Then my friend, the late Miss Chessar —she used, as no doubt you remember, to write for the *Queen*— persuaded me to stand for the London School Board. In prepara- tion for the election she coached me, and I may say that Miss Chessar is the only person who ever taught me anything of business. I was elected, and remained upon the Board for six years. It was in many ways an interesting period to me, and, no doubt, I learnt a great deal. But it was not altogether a pleasant position in which I found myself. Those were the days when women on the School Board were quite a novelty. Several of the ladies held much more advanced views than I did, and—well ! I found it was always my mission to put on the drag. My health, too, gave way towards the end of the time."

THE STORES.

" And was it then that you started these stores ? " I inquired.

" No, I did not start them. They had been opened for about

two years, when, in 1884, I took them over. You must know that I had property already in Bedford Park, and therefore felt an interest in the undertaking, which I thought only needed good management to become extremely successful. But I must admit that for one who knew, as I did, absolutely nothing of trade, it was an enormous undertaking. For the first two years I had the help of a lady partner, but after she left I managed the business entirely alone."

Miss Richardson proceeded to tell me that two years ago the business had been transformed into a limited company, and that she had just lately returned to her former post in order to act as manager on behalf of the shareholders.

THE SYSTEM OF COMMISSION.

From the history of the stores in the past we turned to the stores in the present, Miss Richardson inviting me to make a tour of the departments—fourteen in all. As we roamed through the big building, I noticed at the entrance a post office managed by girls, a well-stocked meat stall, groceries, including pyramids of excellent looking jams, and in a central position stood the flower and fruit stalls. What especially impressed me (looking at the stores with the eye of a would-be customer) was the skill with which the wares were displayed. From the commissionaire at the door, in his smart chocolate-coloured uniform and brass buttons, to the stables where well-groomed horses and neat carts stood ready to convey the customers' goods, everything had that look of orderliness which can only result from conscientious zealous work in all departments. Hearty co-operation can scarcely be obtained without the introduction of the profit-sharing system.

" The head of each department," Miss Richardson explained, "is paid a commission upon his sales in addition to a salary. Some men earn large incomes by their commissions. It is naturally of extreme importance to find able men to control the departments."

At this point in our chat, the head of the wine department kindly offered to show me the cellars, which astonished me by their extent. It was explained to me how the problem of inserting two corks into one bottle could be solved at a touch from an ingeniously contrived machine. Long, cool passages lined with port, claret, and Italian wines showed that the Bedford Park colonists have as pretty a taste in spirituous liquors as in æsthetics.

Having completed the general inspection of the stores, Miss Richardson took me into her own residence, which adjoins the building, and showed me a room there which she had set apart for the *employés* to dine in. She also pointed out that the Stores has for its neighbour the Chiswick School of Arts and Crafts, and told me that this building was also her property.

Then, as I took leave of Miss Richardson, I put one more question to her. Would she, I asked, if the past nine years could be recalled, still do what she had done?

"There have been times," she replied, "when I think that I was rash to take upon myself so vast a responsibility. But I suppose I was born with a tendency towards commercial speculation, and so, if it were to do over again, I should do just the same. And then I have learnt so much of human nature."

There can, I think, be few instances more characteristic of the temper of educated womanhood to-day than this of a lady who has deliberately foregone the supposed delights of wealthy idleness to live laborious, anxious days as a storekeeper.*

---

* Since the autumn of 1893, when the above conversation was recorded, circumstances have altered in one or two important particulars. The principal of these is that Miss Richardson has found her reward for the close personal attention which she was then giving to the Stores; and the fortunes of the business are now re-established on a firm and satisfactory basis. A manager has been appointed, and two gentlemen, well known in the City, share, with Miss Richardson, the responsibilities of the directorate. Relieved from the more arduous duties, which compelled her to reside at Bedford Park, Miss Richardson has latterly made her home at the Lizard, in Cornwall, where she is at present engaged in literary work. Even here, however, her commercial talents have found scope, for she has accepted a place on the directorate of the Housel Bay Hotel, which was opened a year ago. She is likewise a Parish Councillor. But none of these interests have cooled Miss Richardson's affection for her beloved Stores, the welfare of which is still with her a matter of primary concern.

CLERKSHIPS.

MISS CECIL GRADWELL.

IF THERE BE A CREATURE more terrible than the lioness deprived of her cubs, it is the man clerk deprived of his little salary by the woman clerk. I confess frankly that the man clerk in his wrath (notably as evinced in recent newspaper correspondence) inspires me with alarm. I would gladly placate him if possible. If one knew at what precise point of his professional organism he felt sore, it might be possible for woman to pour balm upon his wound. It is understood, for instance, that he feels a tenderness and sense of strain when he hears that women obtain clerkships at lower salaries than himself. This is most natural. Women, too, feel a tenderness on this point, and would only be too happy to oblige him by accepting bigger salaries. But there is a sort of all-overishness about the man clerk's irritation which makes me doubt whether it would be materially salved even if the situation were reversed and women took the bigger salaries and left men to do the underselling. That is why I fear to speak in terms of unsubdued cheerfulness of the success with which Miss Gradwell trains women for clerkships, lest a joyous tone seem to imply callousness for the feelings of a sensitive sex. Nevertheless, the results of the work of Miss Gradwell and her partner, Miss Richardson, are eminently encouraging, and—persiflage apart—will not, I believe, give less satisfaction to the majority of discerning men in the clerical profession than to women.

THE INCEPTION OF THE SCHEME.

It is scarcely two years ago—in the autumn of 1893—that Miss Gradwell and Miss Richardson opened their School of Business Training for Gentlewomen at 5, Victoria-street, West-

minster. Both Miss Gradwell, as an accountant and auditor, and
Miss Richardson, as the director of a Typewriting office, had
already experienced difficulty in obtaining the services of competent women workers in their respective professions : and they
had found that their own experience was that of numerous other
heads of offices. It was evident that some system of training was
urgently needed, and in opening the school Miss Gradwell
declared that the best recompense which she and Miss Richardson
desired was that their pupils should succeed in obtaining
employment of a more skilled, and consequently better paid,
character than that for which they were then fitted. Miss Gradwell
did not wish to add to the number of half-educated typewriting
clerks at starvation wages, and therefore would not seek her pupils
from the half-educated class. But she believed that gentlewomen
of good education and good manners could, if furnished with an
all-round knowledge of business, obtain and hold positions at
fair-wage remuneration.

It was to learn how far this project had been realised at the
end of the twelvemonth that I called again upon Miss Gradwell.
The first evidence my observation yielded was that the suite of
rooms originally occupied by the school had been considerably
enlarged.

Its Realisation.

This note of prosperity was most satisfactorily endorsed by
Miss Gradwell.

" Yes," she said, " You see we have added this room for
typewriting, and another for shorthand, and we shall soon want
more space if pupils increase at the present rate."

" And I am told that you have no difficulty in finding work for
the pupils when they leave ? " " Yes, that is so. I attribute it
partly to my good fortune up to the present in obtaining bright,
intelligent girls. In several instances I have received applications
for pupils the moment their six months' training was completed,
and in one or two cases employers have been wishful to take my
pupils earlier."

The Business Curriculum.

" And the six months' training," I said, " consists of ——? "
" Shorthand," replied Miss Gradwell, " for correspondence

purposes. This subject the pupil learns throughout the six months. Three months cover the shorter course, and the subjects for this are typewriting, book-keeping, and business training. For typewriting we teach both on the Remington and Barlock machines, and book-keeping implies double entry. We have found, that short though a six months' course may seem to be, it is not advantageous to prolong it. Our pupils would at this stage learn far more in three months' practical experience in an office than we could teach them in class lessons."

"But business training is your specialty, I believe, Miss Gradwell?" "Yes, and I must say frankly the business training has been a great success. Many ladies attend the class without any view of becoming clerks, and I think it has been useful to a great many. The classes are held twice a week, one lesson being devoted to private accounts and the ordinary money matters that every woman ought to understand—but I am sorry to say does not—and the other lesson is occupied with general business details. My aim is to teach my pupils what would fit them either to go into an office or to keep the affairs of a wealthy lady in order. I mention duties of the latter kind because I have had personal knowledge of them, having been responsible for the entire conduct of the financial affairs of sundry individuals of large means. But perhaps you would like to see the points we deal with?"

Miss Gradwell then handed me a lengthy syllabus, wherein I noticed many subjects about which we most of us have something to learn. "Writing to and Dealing with Solicitors," "Simple Form of Will," "How to Manage a Banking Account," and "The Meaning of Bankruptcy," offer (the last alone excepted) food for much pleasant reflection to the mind.

CLERICAL AND SECRETARIAL APPOINTMENTS.

Resuming the thread of our talk, I asked Miss Gradwell whether her pupils were obtaining clerkships chiefly in the City. "No," said Miss Gradwell, "because for the present I do not think that City men have much to offer women clerks except work of a mechanical kind. At the same time, I am glad to say that one of our first pupils secured a capital post with a City firm." "What might her salary be?" "At present 35s. a week; later she may get £2." "If she does not marry?" I suggested. "But that is a fatal 'if,' is it not, in these questions of wage, for we hardly ever know what a woman might be earning if she remained at her work into middle life?"

Miss Gradwell regretfully assented, and she followed this line of thought by saying that she did not encourage her pupils to imagine they could earn enough to support themselves immediately on leaving the school; they must be content to take apprenticeship pay at first. But she went on to show that the business training gave her pupils an advantage over unskilled girls, by instancing a well-known firm of gunmakers who had advertised for a short-hand clerk. The advertiser engaged Miss Gradwell's applicant at once, but explained that, as a matter of fact, he did not require shorthand, but had stipulated for this accomplishment in the expectation of obtaining a more competent clerk thereby. In this he was not disappointed, for the young lady possessed a great aptitude for accounts, and, as the drawing up of pay-sheets was one of her principal duties, she at once made herself of value. The firm, in return, have treated her with every consideration. Miss Gradwell was hopeful of finding other clerical openings in solicitors' offices.

I inquired what demand there was for secretaries. "A very fair demand for a certain kind of secretary. Ladies of position require in a secretary one who has been accustomed to the usages of fashionable society. Also they would, I believe, be glad to combine with the secretarial duties the management of their household accounts, and their pecuniary affairs generally. I have known a lady offer from £80 to £100 a year, with residence, for such a secretary, but she never found a woman with the requisite qualifications. Now, this is the kind of lady whose wants we shall be able to meet. But these posts are not, of course, suitable to very young and inexperienced girls. They can only aim at procuring assistant secretaryships, where the responsibility does not fall on their shoulders. There are often posts of this latter kind to be obtained, and they require higher qualifications than a clerkship where the work is mere routine. In the meanwhile we have obtained a good many orders for temporary work. During the season we were asked to recom-mend a young lady who could send out invitations for a very large party. This work was so well done that the hostess paid our nominee 15*s.* a day instead of the customary 7*s.* 6*d.*"

The moral of this conversation, you will perceive, is that there is plenty of well-paid work for capable people. But that has been the moral of all these conversations.

I am forgetting, however, that there is one more word to say; this is, that Miss Gradwell has recently opened a department for the purpose of helping ladies to reclaim Income Tax. I do not think any woman has undertaken this kind of work before. Miss Gradwell is eminently adapted to act as pioneer.

LIBRARIANSHIP.

MISS M. S. R. JAMES.

IF ANY GIRL had asked me within the last few years whether she should become a Librarian, I should have answered, " Try something else." The outlook appeared to me too vague and uncertain. The qualifications were vague, the posts vaguer, the salaries vaguest of all. But I am inclined to think since I had some conversation with Miss James, ex-Librarian of the People's Palace, that this outlook of whilom nebulousness is beginning to assume a form of more pleasing definiteness, and that on the whole we may not do wrong if we encourage a few young women of the right sort to make Librarianships the goal of their ambition.

Perhaps, however, it may seem rather in the nature of a contradiction to say immediately after this that Miss James, when I called upon her,* was just packing up and preparing to leave the Palace, where she had worked first as assistant and afterwards as head Librarian for six years. But the impression was soon conveyed to me that Miss James was far too able and too spirited a person to consider that the hopes of women librarians were to end at the Mile End institution simply because (thanks to the generosity of Mr. Besant and the governors) they had been granted a bright beginning there.

MAKING A FRESH START.

" Yes, I am sorry to say I am leaving the Palace," Miss James acknowledged regretfully, after we had exchanged greetings in her little book-lined office. "We are too severely handicapped for want of funds here nowadays; I can scarcely do any of the

---

* March, 1894.

MISS JAMES.

(From a photograph by Russell and Sons, 17, Baker-street.)

things I should like to do. You see the library has always been a source of great expense, which there is not at present the wherewithal to meet. We have been hoping that the vestry might take it over as a free library, but apparently it will not; meantime, things are at a standstill."

"And you are leaving England, I believe?"—"Yes, I am sailing at once for the United States. I have the offer of a post in the Boston Library Bureau, and I shall take this opportunity of studying the Albany Library School and the library system in the United States generally. But this is not my first visit to the States, you know. I went over in the summer to the Conference of Librarians."

The Position of Women Librarians in the States.

"Is it true that women librarians take a much better position yonder than with us?"—"Oh, certainly they do. To begin with," said Miss James—and I thought the remark noteworthy—"American libraries are altogether in a better position than the generality of our free libraries. I fail to see how, with the system of the library rate grudgingly accorded by the ratepayers, our free libraries are ever to be able to compete with the American libraries, which are handsomely equipped at the cost of the State."—"But ultimately it is the people who pay for the libraries just the same." — "Yes, but the result is somehow more satisfactory"—an answer which I interpreted by thinking that it always is more satisfactory when the rich do not know that they are paying for what they do not want, and the poor for what they would not think they could afford.

"To come back to the women," I continued; "is it true that they all get splendid salaries, and that they never undersell each other?"—"The salaries are distinctly higher, and I do not think underselling is practised, the ordinary rates of remuneration being fixed. Miss Cutler, an authority whose figures I have quoted in a recent paper of my own, mentions that assistants receive from £70 to £180, cataloguers £120 to £180, and for head librarian's work the highest salary paid to a woman is £400. Now these figures represent much better pay than anything we know of here, where £100 is, so far as I know, the most that any woman has received even as head librarian."

I

SALARY DEPENDENT ON CAPACITY AND TRAINING.

"Women librarians are undoubtedly badly off here now; but have you any hope that the position of affairs will mend?" Yes; Miss James was full of hope that it would. "You must remember, however, that the pecuniary question depends on the question of capacity. At present, as for instance in the Manchester Library and its suburban branches, a large number of women are engaged as assistants, at salaries varying, I should say, from £35 to £80. But we do not find women coming forward with quite the ability and the education that would qualify them for the most responsible posts. And if they did come forward, where could they be trained? Hitherto, in the case of the few ladies who beside myself have attempted the higher branches of work, it has been an affair of experiment. We have been drawn towards the profession probably by our love of books, but as to the actual business—the practical routine of librarianship—that we have been obliged to learn as best we might. In my own case, I have derived the greatest advantage from visiting the principal English libraries, and from the helpful advice of such eminent librarians as Dr Garnett, of the British Museum, and Mr. Nicholson, of the Bodleian."

WANTED A SCHOOL FOR LIBRARIANS.

Miss James went on, "What I wish one could see established in this country is a Library School. It is to the training given in the Library School that the American woman owes much of her advantage. The New York State School is the most important; girls who have graduated there are generally sure of a good post, but there are several others existing in connection with libraries, such as Miss Gregor's, at the Drexel Institute, Philadelphia; Miss Sharp's, at the Armour Institute, Chicago; Miss Plummer's, at the Pratt Institute, Brooklyn; and Miss Kelso's, at Los Angeles, California. The mention of the last," added Miss James, smilingly, "reminds me that a Californian lady wrote to me the other day asking how she could become a librarian, and I had the pleasure of telling her that a school existed in her own State."

"Perhaps when you return from America you might set such a school going?" I suggested. "Ah! I can scarcely say anything about that," was the reply. "Possibly such a school may be started in the meantime. I believe the idea has been mooted in connection with Newnham College. If so, it would be very satisfactory. One student from Newnham has lately been working with me here—Miss Petherbridge, and has done excellent work."

WHAT MAKES A GOOD LIBRARIAN.

"Then do I understand, Miss James, that posts would present themselves simultaneously with suitable women?" Miss James assented. "But by suitable women," she explained, "I do not mean only highly educated women of literary tastes. Over and above all this, one must have, in some degree, the kind of capacity that is wanted for running a business successfully. There is a great deal of organising work to be done, as well as correspondence to be transacted; the purchase of books, too, calls for business ability. And although one's time may be very well filled all day, I look upon it as the librarian's first duty to be accessible to everyone who needs her help or advice. Particularly here, at the People's Palace, the librarian can render constant service by recommending books and courses of reading."

And then, as we parted, Miss James said with an emphasis that her vivid, engaging air did not really disguise, "But please let nobody think she can become a librarian as a stop-gap till she marries. It must be undertaken in the spirit of a life-work, or not at all."

INDEXING.

MISS NANCY BAILEY.

WOMEN, possibly because they feel the need of indexes less than men, have scarcely turned their thoughts towards the making of indexes as a profession for themselves. There are not, to the best of my belief, a dozen professional women indexers to be found in the United Kingdom at the present time, perhaps not more than half-a-dozen; but, whatever the precise number may be, I shall not be contradicted in asserting that Miss Nancy Bailey stands, by virtue of her unique position, at the head of her sisters in the profession. For Miss Bailey holds the distinguished appointment of indexer of the Parliamentary Debates, under the contract made with Messrs. Eyre and Spottiswoode. Her appointment is the more flattering to herself because it is, in fact, a re-appointment, Miss Bailey having been indexer for Hansard from 1889 until 1891, when, for one year, the reporting of the Debates passed into the hands of Messrs. Reuter. It shows the satisfactory character of Miss Bailey's work in the Hansard days, that Messrs. Eyre and Spottiswoode should have re-instated her in her former capacity.

Miss Bailey's Professional Career.

But how did Miss Bailey become an indexer, rather than something else? It was a question which I put to Miss Bailey, whom I interrupted in the midst of sorting heaps of neatly inscribed little slips of paper. And a thoughtless enough question too; for the important factor in all successful results of this kind is not that a woman has resolved to become just such and such a thing, but that she has resolved to become something. So it was with Miss Bailey. She could scarcely tell me how she became an indexer. It almost seemed as though she had drifted

(From a photograph by A. Deneulain, Strand.)

into that career. But there had been no drifting when she came
to London from her Shropshire home at the age when most girls
are still at school. That had been a very decisive moment, and
the beginning of a long and a fearless fight for standing-room
amongst the workers. Miss Bailey revealed nothing of the
experiences she had lived through, but imagination and some
knowledge aiding, I could divine that the London paving stones
had been possibly rather stonier to her feet than to others, on
which account, however, her tread had not been the less resolute.
Answering my immediate question, Miss Bailey told me that in
literary work she had made her beginning. She had cared much
about artistic subjects—still cared for them indeed, but indexing
spared her no time for them—and had written upon them in the
magazines. In this connection it came about that she compiled
an index of "The Year's Art." At about the same period she
condensed some two volume novels into one volume, and, among
other work of the kind, she made abstracts of wills for an officer of
the Heralds' College—a dry task and a difficult, but one in which
Miss Bailey's gift for winnowing the wheat from the chaff enabled
her to distinguish herself. It was after one or two trials of this
kind that the editor of Hansard, whom she happened to know,
asked her to index the Parliamentary Debates.

INDEXING HANSARD.

"I shall always remember," said Miss Bailey, " my first start on
Hansard. I felt it was absolutely hopeless; that I should never
succeed. But I worked on, sometimes all day and all night, till
at last I waded through my difficulties. There was nobody to
help me: so I was obliged to evolve my own method."

And presently Miss Bailey explained some points of her method.
She showed me one of the red paper-covered volumes in which
the Debates are published, and, opening it, drew my attention to
the various headings under which the business of the House is
chronicled. These headings, although suitable enough, seen in
connection with the text, would, if taken alone, often convey no
idea of the subject for which the inquirer might be searching. For
instance, supposing that a member of Parliament or journalist
wishes to refer to a question asked by Mr. So-and-so upon a certain topic of the moment. He would look either for the name of

the member who asked the question or for the subject-matter of the question. He would assuredly not think of turning to the phrase " Course of Business," the heading which the reporter has given to the matter. And this instance, as Miss Bailey explained, lets us into the secret of indexing, which is to give the essence of a subject in the fewest and most salient words.

Upon her small slips, then, Miss Bailey inscribes first the names of the members who have spoken, and beneath each name the subjects, in alphabetical order, that the member has spoken on. All these slips having been set in their alphabetical array, the indexer proceeds to make her subject list, and by referring to the name list she can correct mistakes if any arise.   I asked Miss Bailey whether slips of the pen or the mind were not frequent, but she told me she rarely had a complaint, but that errors frequently crept into the printers' proofs, for which reason she makes a point of never correcting proofs without the copy before her.

Opening the Profession to Women.

Miss Bailey originally opened her indexing office (which she has lately removed from Bloomsbury to Westminster) with the intention, especially, of helping women to enter the profession with fewer difficulties than she had herself encountered.   " Indexing is," she explained, " peculiarly suitable for many women because it is essentially a home employment.   But I am sorry to say that, out of more than a hundred applicants for work, I have only found one or two whom I could employ.   One lady, at present, indexes *Pearson's Weekly* under my direction, and another is engaged upon some newspaper cuttings ; but, on the whole, I have found women, however industrious, lack the general knowledge which is required for a good indexer.   I have often felt the want of knowledge myself," she continued ; " and when I began upon the Debates I found myself sadly ignorant of Parliamentary procedure, though I understand it pretty well now.   An index which I had to make upon the Mining Royalties Commission report was puzzling in another way, and demanded a complete technical knowledge of mining terms.   Such words as ' way-leave ' and ' easement,' used sometimes in one signification, sometimes in another, were very troublesome to classify.   Then, again, I have lately been engaged upon fifteen volumes of committee meeting reports of the

Birmingham and Gloucester Canal Company. Here I had to find out, as best I could, what were the subjects of most consequence for reference. These will give you some idea of the expanse of subjects over which the indexer may be expected to range."

I also discovered, in the course of our conversation, that Miss Bailey had indexed Mr. A. W. Hutton's edition of Arthur Young's "Tour in Ireland;" "The Science of International Law," by Mr. Walker, of Peterhouse, Cambridge; a collection of newspaper cuttings for the Shipping Federation, and another for the Liberal Publication Department; Mr. Archbold's work on "The Somerset Religious Houses," and several other books. Letters from the Speaker, the Librarian of the House of Commons, and several of the authors above mentioned testified in unmistakable terms to the value of Miss Bailey's work.

THE INDEXER'S IDEAL.

Can anybody again think of indexing as the mere routine work that the average outsider does think it? He cannot persevere in his ignorance if he realises the ideal of the conscientious labourer in this field. Here is the ideal in Miss Bailey's words: "I build up my index not only for the person who knows what is in the book, but does not know where to find it, but also for the person who does not know what is in the book, and turns to the index to tell him."

Indexing is a profession which, though it must rise in public esteem as our appreciation of exact knowledge increases, is never likely to be remunerated at its absolute worth; but it gives to its votaries a magnificent education, and a sense that the work is of permanent value. Concerning the privilege of indexing the Parliamentary Debates, more than this might be said, even if we do not go quite so far as Mr. Stead, who, congratulating Miss Bailey on her reappointment, wrote:

"For intrinsic importance I would prefer to index Hansard rather than have a seat in the House of Commons. And that important post you have won for womanhood. We all owe you thanks, as human beings, for demonstrating the capacity of woman to do the work—the arduous, responsible work—of actually creating the memory of the Imperial Parliament, session by session. That is noble service which any man might covet, but which it is your peculiar glory to render, being a woman."

It is not for me, however, to gainsay expressions of chivalrous and friendly fervour, which ring all too rarely in the ears of professional women; and without minimising the desirability of a seat in Parliament, we may all cordially agree that the service of Parliament's indexer is "noble service."

JOURNALISM.

JOURNALISM is the most chameleon-like amongst the forms of human activity. It is all things to all men and to all women who practise it—vulgar to the vulgar, sordid to the sordid, prosy to the prosaic, entertaining to the humorous, beautiful to them that love beauty. Hence it is that two persons can no more agree upon a description of journalism than they could upon the appearance of the Emperor's New Clothes. If people's hatreds are stronger than their loves, they find those things they hate in journalism; if people's hopes are stronger than their fears, those hopes, too, are mirrored for them here. So it is, that while one man will tell you that journalism is naught but abomination and desolation, another finds in it the expression of humanity's highest thoughts and aspirations. And, again, journalism expresses the whole man more completely to my thinking than does any other art or profession. It taps his mind at every point, and demands that its tapping should result in a tolerably fertilising stream.

Amongst those who have been good enough to read me so far, I am conscious that there are some of my own calling who are murmuring, " Yes, that is all very fine; but the public ——." Well, let us consider the public. It is such a standing grievance that it is imperative to say a few words concerning it. Now, I fully admit that some of the very greatest human beings in our world's history have had cause to complain of the public, though, as a rule, they have been too great to complain. On the other hand, to complain of the public is not synonymous with greatness. Ninety-nine complainants in the hundred are not great, and they have fallen short—I will not say of greatness, but of fair worldly success by the very defects that lead them to murmur.

In journalism the most frequent occasion of the insuccess for which the public is aspersed is a deficiency either of ideas or of style. Let me explain myself with an instance or two. The journalist who is deficient in ideas is by way of being a person of scholarly and cultivated tastes. She (for I am thinking of women at the moment) happens to read, say, "Two Noble Lives" or Froude's "Letters of Erasmus." "Here," I imagine her saying to herself, "is an improving subject for an article for the readers of the *Bond Street Journal*, whose tastes are so deplorably frivolous." And at once she compiles the paper, consisting of solid slabs of letterpress from the book itself, mortared with an indifferent summary of the text. The article is returned, and provides its compiler henceforth with frequent occasion for quoting the most acrimonious passages about journalism from "Illusions Perdues," and for alluding to Balzac's virtuous young man who lived in a garret, and wrote only for the *cénacle*. But for lack of ideas the thoughtful article runs its scholarly fellow close. Every editor must be familiar with the former; it usually begins somewhat after this fashion: "In these *fin-de-siècle*, 'up-to-date,' days, when women ape the habits of men, and the gentlewomen of the good old time are conspicuous by their absence, when we hear on every hand of 'over-strain' and 'over-pressure,' the writer ventures to offer a few reflections," &c. That is another type of article which finds its way back to the author's sphere of hearth and home, giving rise to observations on the incapacity of the public to apprehend original thought.

Then there is deficiency of style; and by this I would indicate any style that, for one reason or another, cannot be read by an average person of education. Often the style is perfectly grammatical, but it is flat, dull, ineffective. Such a style is only pardonable in one who is unfolding matter of great moment to a small company of experts. But to be consciously tedious when addressing the general public, I hold to be not merely a rudeness but a stupidity. For who can know anything of the lives of his fellow-creatures, with their numberless preoccupations, worries, and interests, without feeling that if people are good enough to attend to him at all, it behoves him to say something that will be interesting to them as well as to himself. To remedy a deficiency of style I have no advice to offer beyond saying that sufferers should confine their offers of contributions as far as possible to the editors of learned societies' journals, and that for the rest they should cultivate their capacity for boredom, which at present is regrettably undeveloped.

To conclude, however, this subject of the public; let us remember that the public, like journalism, is just what we choose to make it. Journalists talk of catering for the servants' hall public when they concoct articles upon what princes have for dinner and what princesses wear; and they believe they are catering for third-class travellers when they sandwich paragraphs about the number of unhanged murderers between free coupons for coffins and wedding rings. And, doubtless, they *have* catered for those folks after a fashion. But this does not prevent other writers catering for the same people in other ways. It does not prevent the servant from reading " Jane Eyre," nor the excursionist from relishing Stevenson. Stevenson and Charlotte Brontë knew something of the heart of man and woman, but they did not know all; and no writer, however great, has yet known all. Ever, as the generations are born and die, there will remain something for the writer to feel and say that other men are feeling and longing to hear said. As for those writers who have nothing to say, or who, having something, are unable to utter it—well, let them admit their own shortcomings. It may be a painful proceeding, but it will at least be modest and dignified.

Under penalty of being thought to protest too much, I would say yet a word about another bugbear which journalists find far less accommodating to their vanity than the " public " bugbear which they fashion for themselves. This bugbear is trotted out when somebody, who does not write for the papers, refers to somebody else who does as "a mere journalist." Now, there is something in that adjective "mere" which arouses the human temper in a more pronounced degree than does the most highly-coloured qualification that has yet received the hall-mark of Billingsgate. What journalistic "mere"-ness is, I am at a loss to say, but I do know, from the tone of the persons who use the word, that it is intended to mean something disagreeable and invidious. The persons in whose mouths I hear the expression most frequently are of two classes. There are certain studious persons (not usually among the most eminent) who are secretly annoyed if the public does not understand their work, and openly annoyed when anyone succeeds in explaining it. As the interpreter not uncommonly reduces the product of many years' complicated toil to a few short-syllabled words, the studious one is vexed : hence the " mere "-ness. The other disparaging person may be a novelist (also not in the first flight), or a person who writes occasionally for a monthly magazine. Individuals of this type have reasons of their own for disparaging journalists who also happen to be critics : hence, again, this " mere "-ness.

Do not suppose, however, that I wish to hold up the profession of journalism as being without speck or blemish. There is an unsightly side to it—nay, I might say it has more than one unsightly side. Indeed the frontage which it presents to the new-comer must commonly appear ugly, though rarely, as it would seem, so ugly as to dissuade from entrance. About the doors hang a loafing crowd of plausible rascals, who easily outwit the inexperience of a girl. If the girl possess money and ambition, there is always some swindling fellow ready to rob her of the one on pretence of satisfying the other ; if she be pretty and poor other dangers await her ; and if she be poor but not pretty there is always some quick-witted exploiter of human labour alert to rob her of her little capital of youthful ideas and energy, and to offer the victim for her accommodatingness what the exploiter terms experience and the exploited mental exhaustion.

But if the adventures of these stumblers on the threshold are painful to witness, I do not know that we shall receive more pleasure by watching the doings of those wayfarers who succeed in setting foot inside the palace of journalism, but often get no further than the ante-hall. The women of this party are engaged at best upon some extremely uninteresting tasks, and at worst upon some discreditable ones. If we could look over shoulders, we should find dull ladies making paste-and-scissor *réchauffés* of stale news, or writing such unnecessary statements as that, " On the 29th ult. the forty-third annual meeting of the Retrogressive Society was held at Reporters' Hall, World's End," &c. Other ladies, dressed according to the moment's extra special edition of the fashions, are inditing gushing " Girls' Letters," into which they introduce such detailed descriptions of the entire stock-in-trade of Messrs. Blouse and Madame Aigrette (including the full com-mercial style and postal address of the firms in question), as make the gushing girl appear extraordinarily like the pushing salesman. Whether there is an even greater resemblance between characters ostensibly so foreign to each other we will not too narrowly inquire. The *Times* permitted some light to be thrown on the matter not long since. Yet another company consists of jaded-looking fashionable women, who are trying to pay their dressmakers' bills by writing about the private parties they have been to, and the unwise things that they heard said in friendly confidence.

Well, well; such is the ante-chamber. I would not tarry in it for an instant were it not that there are those who contend that women are compelled to spend their days in this brain and soul-deadening locality. Time was, perhaps, when women were compelled by the editorial expectancy that amounts to compulsion, to write only gossip, fashions, and cookery. And yet, as the thought comes to me of Miss Martineau's important articles, and of Miss Cobbe's daily leaders, I feel that my statement is belied. It is so easy to say "time was" when we mean to arrange that to-day shall beat the record. Leaving historical comparison, then, to the students, and looking only at those things of to-day which we have the means of appreciating, I think we shall find that feminine ability is not handicapped in journalism after the manner that croaking observers would have us believe.

Circumstances, as I see them, are extraordinarily in our favour. Quick-witted editors are eager to obtain the woman's view of life, so long as that view can be expressed in fair English. And they are quite right. The newspapers of thirty years ago may or may not have been ideal prints—there are persons audacious enough to say they were not—but they failed to treat of almost anything that women cared about. The average woman, when reading them, felt almost as much an outsider as a young girl does who finds herself at table with a party of old gentlemen. They were permeated, those good old papers, with an intolerable atmosphere of fogey-dom, and consequently were eschewed, I venture to think, by all women whose minds were not of the most "nobly planned" order. The editor of to-day, fulfilling the primary duty of enlarging his paper's circulation, takes care not to forget women. Indeed, if he be clever, he will more readily forget men. For the (numerically) greater include the (numerically) less. If a woman can read a paper—not a fashion paper—from cover to cover without being bored, a man may be guaranteed to read the same paper with a sense of quite hilarious entertainment. For women who suffer bores gladly in lecture halls, drawing-rooms, and elsewhere, become intensely sensitive to their objectionableness in the press. Wherefore the well-advised journalist, in the course of his writing, will ask himself occasionally: " Supposing I were saying these things to my partner at a dinner table, would she at this point be looking at me with a bright eye and appreciative smile, or would she be turning towards me a diminishing profile ? " And while he can fancy her smile at its gayest he will stop.

A woman journalist has the advantage that she need ask herself no such questions. She is her own thermometer of tedium. Sometimes, I confess, she neglects to apply the thermometer, because she is thinking of the piece-rate. This is a short-sighted policy. But on the whole, if it be the affair of the journal to go home to men's business and bosoms, it is an affair that its feminine contributor thoroughly understands. She imports into her work conversational ideas and the conversational method. " Yes ; she is detestably colloquial," says somebody of the Old Guard. She is colloquial, certainly. I suspect that most of those "ancients," whom we read with any satisfaction now, were thought "detestably colloquial " by the Old Guard of their time. The Old Guard prefer newspaper English. I make them a present of it to have and, in their clemency, to withhold, including all those ornamental fitments and garnishings of " choice exotics," " feathered songsters," " succulent bivalves," and "well-chosen words " in general.

It will be reckoned that I have only dealt with my subject in an unpractical, up-in-the-clouds way if I do not address a few words specifically to the beginner. Anything, however, which I might dare to say to her is only the corollary of what has gone before. I would say, then, this:

" Make up your mind in the first instance that writing is the work you care most about; that you love the music of language ; and that to put your individual thought into the form that best fits it affords you the highest possible pleasure. Then, having resolved this question, put the ideal aside for a while, and only treat yourself to an occasional peep at it, for you have to go to business, and just at the outset the business and your ideal will not seem to have very much in common. If you live out of

London and the literary world, as most beginners who need advice do, there are several negative injunctions I would impose. One is never to answer advertisements that offer inexperienced people editorships and the like on condition of a pecuniary investment. These short cuts to success generally end in quicksands. Another short cut that I would dissuade you from taking is to write long and lofty articles on, shall we say, " The Relations of the Sexes," for the most distinguished monthly magazines. You will not be aware of it, but you will probably only say trite things in an amateurish manner, and your MS. will return to be watered with your tears. Thirdly, do not write about places ; for ideas are not in places but in the people who live in them.

And now—for I cannot bear to find myself *ein Geist der stets verneint*—I will be affirmative. Begin, I would say, by sending tiny paragraphs of news to one paper and another. See to it that the news is such as may legitimately be published, word it dexterously, freshly, and grammatically, and send it off without the loss of a single post. Gradually you will find that your news is acceptable to certain papers. Continue sending to those papers so systematically that the editors recognise they may depend upon you. Beware at this point of imposing on editorial good nature by sending any news that is not of first-rate importance. One day something of national interest will happen in the country town, where I am assuming you live, and you may be privileged to supply the description. Meantime you have been carefully studying the idiosyncrasies of the best papers, and by-and-bye you will pluck up courage to send something that shall be more ambitious than your paragraphs and reports. It may—this article I am thinking of—embody some personal investigation or inquiries into a subject of consequence, or it may be a light, sprightly affair—half essay, half story. If you succeed with work of one or other of these kinds, your adviser may say good-bye to you, and wish you well. For you have now only to make the most of the opportunities that will come to you, if, that is to say, you have meanwhile migrated to London, as I take for granted you will have done.

It were well, too, that at this juncture you should take the exalted literary ideal of your girlhood from its hiding-place. It will only be your own fault now if you do not come somewhere within sight of it. Some of your journalistic friends will assure you of the reverse; that it is editors and the public who forbid you to realise it, who compel you to be not the literary but the " mere " journalist. Do not believe them. Refer the question instead to your own memory. Recollect the articles that came back on your hands. Were they not either lamentably ill-written or wanting in tact and persuasiveness towards the fellow-creatures whom you wished to address? For nearly all the writers of good English who fail, come to grief because they forget that they are talking to anybody except themselves. And what of the good articles that were published? Were they ever a quarter so good as you saw them written on your brain before your pen played you its tricks? And what of the articles that you have thought of writing, or that you have even been asked to write and have not written? Where are they, and why are they unwritten? Because they were too good and great for papers and public? Not at all. Because you could not write them."

That is where I touch the one great disappointment of all literary effort. Every day brings with it a new opportunity to efface from the memory the scar of an old failure. But with every opportunity that we cannot take we are wounded by the sense of our own feebleness and ineptitude. In the course of a journalistic experience that has extended over some years I have frequently been counselled to "put pride in my pocket," and although I have found myself habitually indisposed to relegate pride to any such place of seclusion, I confess that the discipline of literary inability and incompetence has not left much pride to be disposed of anyhow.

It is impossible, however, to close upon a note of lamentation. In journalism women have a more assured position than in almost any of the great arts and professions. Between women and men in it there is no question of rights, and, I trust, very little of rivalry. If proof were needed of the good fellowship that exists, it is found in the absolute equality of treatment meted out to both sexes by the Institute of Journalists. On the social side, the Writers' Club affords opportunities for pleasant interchange of ideas such as women do not, so far as I can learn, enjoy in almost any other calling. And I must not forget the economic circumstances which are at the root of this reasonable equality. Journalism gives a beginning salary of from £50 to £100 a year to many a girl who elsewhere would be paying as much for a college education or an apprenticeship premium. To women of more ability it gives an income that rises from £200, £300, and £400 to an unknown maximum. There are many who think such incomes hardly earned. I cannot say I am one of them. Mental and physical wear and tear, drudgery, sometimes anxiety, there are, I quite admit; but people cannot expect to be paid for nothing. But along with the exertion comes such a quickening of the pulses, such an awakening of the brain, such a sense of being carried along upon the rushing torrent of human life as make me ofttimes disposed to marvel that payment should be offered for accepting a gift that is without price. This last too candid admission is not, however, I beg leave to say, intended to be observed by editors.

K

THE HOME LIFE OF
PROFESSIONAL WOMEN.

THERE IS A SHORT WAY of dealing with this subject.
I might say, "There is no home life for professional
women," and in so saying I should not merely comply with my
own indolence, but should express the thought—or the wish,
which is often much the same thing—of a large number of
people. For to the majority of family folks no illusion is dearer
than the pitiability of the professional woman's lot. They gloat
over their illusion, they shake their heads over it, they talk over it.
And the worst of it is that their talk gets to the ears of the subject
of their compassion. Now, compassion acts like a strong poison
upon those who have no need of it; and only those with
the stoutest mental constitution can withstand its peculiarly
penetrating and convincing quality. The happiest and busiest
spinster in the world, if compassionated for her lot by a woman
bound to a tedious husband and a family of troublesome children,
will feel that the integrity of her bliss has suffered some damage.
For she cannot rid herself of the compassion by handing it back
to the domesticated donors (as it is the first impulse of her heart
to do) lest she wreak havoc in many a peaceful family circle. Since
it is tacitly understood that, except in the abstract or in farce, the
unmarried may never commiserate the married: on the other
hand, the married may freely pour compassion upon the unmarried, and are, indeed, encouraged to hold themselves public
benefactors for so doing.

Now the professional spinster—I do not concern myself with
the professional married woman who admittedly has the best of
both worlds—is condoled with on many things, but the chief
among these is loneliness. "You must be so lonely living by
yourself" is the chronic ejaculation of persons who have never

looked out on the world with their own eyes, thought their own thoughts, or made their own acquaintance. " And you must be so dreadfully dull in the evening," add these devotees of round games and reading aloud. The professional woman, returning to her own place after a long day's work and much intercourse with her fellows, had been immensely happy to rest in the evening with her feet on the fender, a newspaper and novel by her side. But the mention, the frequent mention, of this word loneliness has its corrosive effect upon her being. She convinces herself at last that true happiness—the other was only a first-rate imitation—must be found in life at close quarters with a large number of persons. So she becomes sure that she is very lonely.

The spinster's table is the next point to which the domesticated direct their attack. The gospel of chops and steaks is preached unintermittently by matrons with a secret hankering for Bath buns and gingerbeer; and occasionally the matrons take the spinster home to taste the joys of the nursery leg of mutton and rice pudding, and be converted. But the spinster, though not converted, is convinced—convinced, that is, that she does live very meagrely, and that it beseems her forlorn state so to live. Consequently she drops the butcher's acquaintance, bestows all her favours on the greengrocer and the applewoman, is careful to forget her lunch, and makes an aerated tea her dinner. Thus she strives to realise the ascetic ideal that her friends have been good enough to form.

But the lone woman has still to acquiesce in one or two other beliefs. She must bring herself to perceive that with an income of a couple of hundreds and an exact forecast of her expenses, she is worse off than her sister the matron, whose share in her husband's four hundred is chronically anticipated for children's clothes and doctor's bills. She finds it difficult to bring her almost morbid scrupulosity about money matters into harmony with the theory of insolvency; but she may compass it by a loan to the family sinking fund of her married relative.

And then last, but in the eyes of women first, is the social grievance. " Without a gentleman," says the suburban matron, in her most sympathetic tone, " you cannot hope to entertain "— nor, she implicitly assumes, to be entertained. And our spinster, if she is foolish enough to imagine that the highest joys of human intercourse are achieved when half a score of ill-assorted couples meet round a board, shyly abandons her projected friendly lunch or octave dinner.   She lapses instead into strictly feminine afternoon teas; and lest these should wax too hilarious, she announces on the card of invitation that the gathering will partake of the nature of a symposium, or that one lady will address everybody else upon her " Work."

Now I am aware that there are persons (not necessarily themselves married) who hold that the professional spinster ought to be driven to abandon her profession and her spinsterhood by sheer domestic dreariness and discomfort.   It is not long ago that a lady, prominent in the educational world, was horrorstruck at the hedonic images evoked in her mind by the sight of a pretty tea-set in a young spinster's rooms.   From her remarks on the subject she led us to infer that a man who could not offer his sweetheart a set of tea things as the exclusive paraphernalia of matronhood would stand no chance in offering himself.   I am not yet disposed to believe that marriage is reduced to so parlous a plight, nor that we shall increase the number of happy marriages by inaugurating a system of spinsters' suttee.

With the persons who preach spinsters' suttee I am not minded to argue, for I can meet them on no common ground.   But the spinsters who incline their ear to such teaching I would gladly turn from their error.   I would say to them, " Inasmuch as you are women, you have in yourselves all the gifts of domestic life. If you were bachelors you might reasonably complain; they have not these gifts, yet, as a matter of fact, they seldom bemoan their fate.   If you need companionship, invite another spinster to join you, only making up your mind in advance whether your partner is to play first or second fiddle in the establishment.   For, though two second fiddles may make passable domestic melody, the union of two first fiddles results in terrible discord.   Take, then, a flat in a central situation (which will be far more attainable by friends than the distant villas of large family circles), and engage a teachable cook and parlourmaid."

" But," I think one of the ascetically-minded interposes, " I should feel too selfish living in all this comfort.   Anything would do for me."   To which I reply, " Your nicely (but not expensively) managed home will not benefit you only.   It will be a school of training for your servants, whose needs you must make it your business to know and sympathise with. It will be an oasis of peace to numbers of people in trouble and perplexity. The married woman cannot compete with you here, in her home distracted with family cares. You can give to each comer an undivided attention, and be sure you avail yourself of the privilege.

"And then about that difficulty of entertaining. It is no difficulty really, but a mere matter for courage and discretion. Recognise that frumpishness and Bohemianism are your Scylla and Charybdis, and steer your course between. Thus you will be able to give some charming parties. You have one great advantage over the ordinary woman with the visiting list—nobody expects the smallest hospitality from you. And should you disappoint this expectation by offering your guests a sociable, well-cooked, properly served little meal, so that someone says privately afterwards, 'Upon my word Miss Smith understands how to do things!' is there any great harm in that? Should not the art of the home be your chief accomplishment?"

It were vain to hope that an admonition such as this would produce much effect. Many other and more powerful exhortations are needed before we can shake the conviction that by leading a temporary and hugger-mugger existence in the celibate condition women are proving their power to gladden and irradiate the matrimonial hearth. All roads lead to the altar; and it is possible, since the advocates of matrimony induce us so to believe, that the tea-cupless spinster come quickest to the goal. But her short route takes her *via* a home that may be likened to Clapham Junction for its discomfortable air, its unwilling sojourners, and hasty departures. The professional woman, who, I frankly concede, is often in no hurry to reach the bourne, has my sympathies when she chooses the longer way in order to enjoy the journey as she goes.